Getting In:

Insider Tips on College Admissions for Immigrant Families

BY
DANIEL BYUN

ISBN: 978-1-257-91695-5

Introduction

Applying to colleges has always been an intense and anxiety-ridden rite of passage for high school seniors across the U.S. But things have recently reached fever pitch: every fall, we hear of record-breaking numbers of applicants; every spring, an ever-shrinking percentage of these applicants find a spot at one of the top-tier schools. It's hard to imagine how the process could get any tougher, and yet it does, year after year.

In fact, things have gotten so ultra-competitive that decisions can often seem arbitrary. Why does one valedictorian waving a 4.0 and 2400 get admitted, while another does not? For even the best-informed, the college process can be unpredictable and baffling. How much more so for immigrant families with cultural and language barriers to overcome!

Over the last several years, I've seen too many of these immigrant families get waylaid by misinformation and bad advice. These bright, hardworking students and their devoted parents end up wasting valuable time, money and energy, making poor decisions with lasting consequences.

This book is written for just such families: for "1.5" and second-generation immigrant students and their parents. I aim to demystify the college admissions process in the belief that an accurate understanding of what colleges really look for and value in candidates is the key to navigating the process successfully.

Chapter one gives an overview of the college admissions process. Chapters two through five take a closer look at each of the four key components of the college application: the high school transcript (grades and courses), the standardized test record (SATs or ACT), extracurricular activities and, finally, personal essays and recommendations. Chapter six offers tips for choosing the right college, making sure that students understand how broad and diverse their options really are. In chapter seven, I provide specific guidelines for students at different stages of their high school careers. Finally, in chapter eight—but also throughout the book—we work through several case studies. Although names and some identifying details have been changed, these are real-life stories that I hope will not only illustrate the book, but also motivate and encourage students...even, if necessary, warn them about the potential consequences of their choices.

The good news? Students who have yet to put in their college applications still have *something* left that they can do to take control of the admissions process and influence the outcome.

*   *   *

Before getting started, I should introduce some terminology. Throughout this book, I talk about "top-tier" and "second-tier" schools, as well as "most selective," "more selective," and "selective" schools. What do these terms mean?

"Top-tier schools" are the top twenty-five universities in the *U.S. News & World Report*'s annual National Universities rankings *plus* the colleges in the top fifteen spots the Liberal Arts Colleges rankings.[1] (These lists are partially reproduced in Appendices I-III of this book for ease of reference.) "Second-tier" schools round out the top fifty.

The "most selective" schools are the Ivy League schools plus Stanford, Williams College, Amherst College, MIT, Caltech and a

---

[1] "National University Rankings 2011" and "National Liberal Arts College Rankings 2011." *U.S. News & World Report.* 17 Aug 2010.

few other institutions. All of these schools accept less than 15% of applicants. "More selective" schools are the rest of the "top-tier" schools; all schools in the top two tiers are "selective." (Note that selectivity is only one of several factors that go into determining rankings, so not all of the top ten most selective schools are ranked in the top ten overall.)

The following table should help clarify these terms:

Top Tier	Most selective	Ivy League
Top Twenty-Five National Universities *plus* Top Fifteen Liberal Arts Colleges	≤ 15% accepted	Stanford, MIT, Caltech Williams, Amherst, Pomona, etc.
	More selective	University of Chicago, Northwestern, Duke, Johns Hopkins, etc.
Second Tier Rest of Top Fifty	**Selective**	University of Michigan, Boston College, NYU, Colgate, Smith, etc.

Although these terms will come in handy, let me say now what I will emphasize again and again in pages to come: students should not put too much weight on these rankings! They can be helpful tools in the admissions process, but the best college for a particular student will not always—or even often—be the highest-ranked college he or she gets into. Just as every student is a unique individual, so every college offers a unique set of opportunities in a unique environment. Getting the right fit between student and college is a complex matter, which is why it's going to take us a book to help students navigate the process and secure the best options for themselves. With that important warning in place, let's get started with an overview of the college admissions process.

Chapter 1:
The College Admissions Process

1.1 The Spirit of College Admissions

Over the last two decades, the contest to get into a "good" college has escalated to the point where it is now practically a competitive sport...and the intensity of the process shows no signs of abating. Part of the problem lies in the sheer quantity of applicants: in 2009, an unprecedented 3.32 million students graduated from U.S. high schools.[2] But a bigger part of the problem lies in the quality of these graduates. In recent years, nearly half of all American college-bound seniors graduated with a grade point average of A– or above.[3] These students, fueled by ready access to college counseling and test prep, are performing at superstar levels.

Compounding the problem for immigrant families is the prevalence of myths or false information about the admissions

---

[2] U.S. Census Bureau. "School Enrollment, Faculty, Graduates, and Finances—Projections: 2009 to 2015." *Statistical Abstract of the United States: 2011.* Washington: Government Printing Office, 2010.

[3] U.S. Department of Education. "SAT Mean Scores of College-Bound Seniors, by Selected Student Characteristics: Selected Years, 1995-96 through 2008-09." *Digest of Education Statistics 2009.* Washington: National Center for Education Statistics, 2010.

process. Part of this misunderstanding is cultural. In Asia, for example, the main criterion for college admissions is academic achievement. In this regard, the Asian admissions culture is most similar to that of *public* U.S. universities such as the UCs (I'll discuss this more later). However, grades and test scores do not even begin to account for the complexities of the *private* school application process in the U.S.

Misunderstandings about college admissions are also fueled by ill-informed anecdotal sources: the experiences of friends and family members as well as the counsel of misguided persons. The Vice-President of Enrollment at Dickinson College, a prestigious liberal arts college in Pennsylvania, worried about this very issue to the *New York Times*. "It's really accelerated in the past year to the point where there is a ton of bad information out there," he said. "People need to realize that anybody can say anything on the Internet."[4]

Before students start looking for a hard and fast set of rules, however, they must try to grasp the *spirit* of the college admissions process. Essentially, academics are only a part of the picture. Many people assume that the stronger the academic record (the higher the test scores and GPA), the more likely a candidate is to be admitted. However, this isn't necessarily the case. The admissions process is much more multifaceted. For most schools, but especially for private schools, academic achievements are only a minimal criterion for admission. Each college then uses its own set of values and requirements to create its ideal freshmen class. As Lee Stetson, former Dean of Admissions at the University of Pennsylvania, once noted, "Eighty-five percent of those who apply [to U Penn] would thrive here, but we have to choose among them. *We're not looking for only the best numbers.*"[5]

---

[4] Saulny, Susan. "College Admission Angst Finds a Forum on Web." *New York Times*. 31 Mar 2006.

[5] Peterson's College Search. "College Acceptance: Making the Final Cut." Web. 18 Feb 2011.

This means that admissions is as much an art as it is a science. It is neither entirely subjective nor precisely predictable. Of course, there are quantifiable and comparable academic achievements: GPA and SAT (or ACT) scores, most importantly. But these numbers alone do not account for admissions results. Every application is assessed for its merits along four further dimensions: (i) extracurricular activities, (ii) the personal statement (college essay), (iii) teacher and counselor recommendations and (iv) the interview (when offered). (There are also factors affecting admissions decisions that are independent of the merits of particular applicants. These include things like demographic concerns and the particular culture of a school. We will see how these factors come into play in some of our case studies.)

To see where the science of college admissions ends and the art of it begins, consider this helpful illustration from Jon Reider, former Senior Admissions Officer at Stanford University.[6] Stanford received a record 34,200 applications to the Class of 2015.[7] Picture all these applications scattered on the floor of the Stanford admissions office. Now applicants who are academically qualified for admission—those whose GPA and SAT/ACT scores meet minimal criteria—will get picked up off the floor and brought to the table. The number of academically qualified applicants may be about 23,000. Of the students who make it to the table, a further 20,600 will get cut, leaving around 2,400 acceptances. Once applications make it to the table, academic numbers don't come into play again, *unless a student's test scores and GPA are far above the average for the school.* For a school like Stanford, which maintains extremely stringent academic requirements, it's more or less impossible for a student's scores to be significantly above average. Therefore, the only way for an applicant to get accepted is for the rest of his

[6] Reider, Jon. In personal conversation.

[7] "Undergraduate applications to Stanford continue to rise." *Stanford Report.* 13 Jan 2011.

or her application profile to be very strong. In other words, once students pass the initial, "scientific" part of the evaluation process, things become much more of an "art." At this point, colleges are looking for what students will bring to the school community and how well they will fit together with each other and the culture of the school.

Of course, Stanford isn't exactly the norm. There are many great colleges that attract applicant pools with more readily attainable academic achievements. Applicants with extra-ordinary academic records may be able to get into such schools on the strength of their numbers alone: they enjoy an advantage because colleges can use their achievements to boost admissions statistics and hence rankings. However, above-average grades and test scores are no guarantee of admission, not even at the less-competitive schools.

There is one crucial message for students to take to heart from these introductory remarks. There is a strong trend among students to apply to "reach" schools: schools with higher academic averages than those attained by the student. This trend is particularly strong among immigrant families. The reality that students must come to terms with is that the applicant sitting at the lower end of a school's academic range—the student, for example, with a 2150 on the SAT, applying to a school where incoming freshmen attain an *average* score of 2250—will almost certainly *not* get in, *unless the student has something truly outstanding in a non-academic area to compensate for the below-average academics.*

In the following chapters, I'll use this information to analyze case studies of real-life students who applied to a variety of colleges, public and private. I'll also answer frequently asked questions, including, How many AP courses should students take? What SAT score is good enough? What is a good extracurricular activity? Before turning to these specific issues, however, I'll introduce some general trends in college admissions. I'll also dispel some popular but harmful misconceptions that are widespread in the immigrant community.

1.2 General Trends in College Admissions

As a college counselor who sees lots of high school seniors navigate the admissions process year after year, I get to spot some general trends. Analyzing data from the high school class of 2011 early admission candidate pool, I've identified four of the most important.

1. GPA remains the most important academic factor in determining admission.

2. SAT/ACT scores are becoming less important.

3. Students must deploy a focused application strategy.

4. Essays and interviews are becoming more important.

GPA remains the most important factor

Earning good grades in rigorous courses is still the most important factor in college admissions, and for a very good reason: school performance over a period of years is the best indicator of whether or not a student will be academically successful at the college level. Having the proven capacity to achieve at a particular college is a baseline requirement just to *qualify* for entrance to that college. The bar is set higher or lower depending on the school and the average achievements of applicants to the school, and most schools will not, at least publicly, specify a "cut-off" score. As I explained above, once this minimal academic standard has been met, students will be in the running for admission and non-academic factors will come into play. However, students who have everything going for them *except* academics—students with fantastic extracurricular activities and accomplishments, but without the grades and scores to prove that they will be successful in their college studies—will *not* be considered for admission.

It is important to understand that colleges don't think of the GPA as a mere overall number. Rather, they read a student's transcript to see what academic choices the student has made and what these choices say about the student's character. A desirable candidate demonstrates intellectual curiosity by taking the most rigorous courses available. An *ideal* candidate thrives in these challenging courses and maintains a high GPA despite the difficulty of his or her coursework. By contrast, the applicant who habitually chooses to take a "regular" class when there are AP options available reveals a lack of either the ability or the motivation necessary to flourish in a competitive college environment. Therefore, the selection of courses is as important as performance.

Remember: even if a high GPA alone cannot guarantee admission into a private college, a low GPA can guarantee a rejection.

SAT/ACT scores are becoming less important

The debate over the merits and demerits of the SAT, the most popular standardized test for undergraduate admissions, is a long-standing one. New York University (NYU) made head-lines when it recently eliminated the SAT requirement altogether,[8] but it is only the highest profile member of an ever-growing list of colleges taking this bold step. Wake Forest University (ranked 25th in the 2011 *U.S. News & World Report* listings) is the top-ranked university to drop the SAT requirement.[9] Several top-ten liberal arts colleges, including Middlebury College (ranked 4th) and Bowdoin College (ranked 6th) have also made this move.[10]

Nevertheless, it remains important for applicant SAT or ACT scores, when submitted, to fall within the average range of the target school. And it is still true that an exceptionally strong score can help a student secure admission, although it will not do as much as an excellent GPA.

---

[8] Hoover, Eric. "New York U. Plans to Make ACT and SAT Scores Optional for Applicants." *Chronicle of Higher Education.* 20 Apr 2009.

[9] "National University Rankings 2011." *U.S. News & World Report.* 17 Aug 2010. For a comprehensive list of colleges for which the SAT is optional, see the FairTest website (http://www.fairtest.org/university/optional).

[10] "National Liberal Arts College Rankings 2011." *U.S. News & World Report.* 17 Aug 2010.

Good performances on other standardized exams can also make a difference. The SAT Subject Tests and the AP Exams help to highlight academic interests and demonstrate special strengths. Students applying to top colleges as engineering majors, for example, should take the Math 2 and Physics or Chemistry SATs. They should also strongly consider taking AP courses and exams in these subjects. And if a student does not score well on the Critical Reading or Writing sections of the SAT, performing highly on an English or History SAT or AP can help compensate. As a matter of fact, in lieu of the SAT or the ACT, NYU currently accepts one of the two following combination of tests:

- three SAT Subject Test scores (one in the humanities, one in math or science, and one non-language subject of the student's choice) OR

- three AP Exam scores (one in the humanities, one in math or science, and one non-language subject of the student's choice).[11]

A focused application strategy is crucial

When students apply to colleges, their task is to show who they are and how they are different from other students. A carefully developed application strategy is crucial to accomplishing this. A case study will help introduce this idea.

When I met Tim, he was a junior hoping to attend one of the most selective universities as an engineering major. Tim maintained perfect grades and a well-rounded extracurricular profile through the end of his sophomore year, all while attending one of California's most competitive public high schools and participating in a good number of science-oriented activities (Robotics Club, a summer engineering internship, etc.). At the beginning of his junior year, his goals seemed attainable. However, in the first semester of junior year, Tim earned Bs in

---

[11] New York University Admissions Office. "Standardized Tests." Web. 14 Feb 2011.

core engineering classes—AP Calculus BC, AP Physics and AP Computer Science—though he attained As in AP U.S. History and Honors English.

Could Tim still target the most selective universities as an engineering major? Unfortunately, probably not. Tim's high school was known for its unusual strengths in math and science. As a result, Tim was surrounded by classmates with equally good extracurricular profiles who were also targeting Ivy League schools as engineering majors. And many of these students earned solid As in AP Calculus BC, AP Physics, and AP Computer Science, the very classes that gave Tim trouble. Since GPA is the most important factor in admissions, Tim's Bs significantly decreased his chances of getting admitted to the most selective schools as an engineering student.

Tim still had a shot at Ivy League colleges as a *non*-engineering major. This would, however, require a significant shift in application strategy—a decision not to be made lightly. A change of application strategy affects course selection, test selection and target test scores, summer activities, essay topics…even the choice of teachers to write recommendations.

So Tim had a tough decision to make. Should he target Ivy-level schools as a non-engineering major or should he shift his attention to other colleges where he could study engineering, though at the expense of brand name?

Note that although colleges do not generally require students to declare majors until the end of sophomore year, they do consider an applicant's *intended* major when assessing his or her academic and extracurricular record.

It is also important to know that many universities have separate colleges for the humanities and for engineering. Students are admitted to a specific college, and different colleges can have different requirements and sometimes significantly different admission rates. (For example, in 2011, Carnegie Mellon admitted 30% of applicants to College of Humanities and Social Sciences but only 14.2% of applicants to the School of Computer

Science.[12]) Although it is sometimes possible to switch colleges after matriculating, there is no guarantee that such internal transfers will be permitted.

Now in Tim's case, we recommended that he continue to pursue his long-standing goal of applying as an engineering major. Not only was engineering Tim's clear area of interest, but changing direction as a junior would have been risky. Tim had been prioritizing math and science courses and choosing extracurricular activities with an engineering focus through-out his high school career. Shifting application strategy would have destabilized the coherence of Tim's "identity."

Let us now generalize from the case of Tim to see what a focused application strategy does. Applying for college is like applying for a job. When seeking a position within a specific company, a job-seeker must tailor his or her résumé as closely as possible to match the job being applied for. In the same way, students must be strategic in writing their applications. From matters small (the ordering of items on a list of activities) to large (the choice of essay topic), an applicant must present a coherent self-portrait of a student who will fit in at a particular school.

Essays and interviews are becoming more important

Remember that getting into college is an art as much as a science. Two key components falling under the first heading are essays and interviews. Both provide opportunities for students to express their unique personalities and share their passions. They allow students to show parts of themselves that are not on display anywhere else in the application.

The selection of essay topic is a critical part of an application strategy. Although many colleges use their own essay prompt, all of the topics essentially boil down to the same elemental question: "Who are you?" Obviously, nobody can *fully* answer

---

[12] Carnegie Mellon Undergraduate Admission. "Admission Statistics." Web. 17 Feb 2011.

this question, least of all in a 500-word essay! But for colleges, getting *some* sense of an applicant's identity is crucial. After all, when a student matriculates into a college, he or she will be someone's roommate, someone's classmate, someone's student. Colleges look for students who will complement the school culture, fit into the social fabric of a school, and make meaningful contributions to community life. Now for most college applicants—and for all applicants who have done due diligence in constructing a focused application strategy—essay topics should emerge readily from extracurricular experiences. It is important for students to see their essays as opportunities to reveal something new about themselves, *not* to re-present their résumés in paragraph form! Essays are a lens through which colleges can see what a student's values are, how the student sees and reacts to the world, etc.

What the essay does in written form, the interview does in person. And just as essays must be drafted and re-drafted before being submitted, so, too, students must prepare for the admission interview. There are two key questions that interviewers will ask. The first question, once again, is "Who are you?" In developing and deploying an application strategy, students will have grappled with this question in many different forms. If they have done their work properly, then they will have no problem knowing how to answer this question. The second key question is, "Why do you want to come to my school?" Answering this question successfully requires research and preparation. Students must have a knowledgeable and *school-specific* answer to this question up their sleeve.

In this section, I presented four of the most important *general* trends affecting college admissions. In the next section, I'll highlight a few developments that have specifically affected the University of California (UC) admissions process.

1.3 Trends in College Admissions: UCs

There are three major factors affecting UC admissions practices:

1. New policies have been put in place that will make it increasingly difficult for applicants from immigrant families, especially Asian families, to gain admission.

2. The California state budget crisis has had an impact on enrollment at the UCs.

3. Tuition hikes have begun to close the gap between UC and private college costs of attendance.

New admissions policies

California is one of the most diverse regions of the world. The state has the largest minority population in the U.S.[13] However, comparing *state* demographic data with the demographics of the *California public college student population* shows a significant disparity. For example, Asians account for 12% of California's population.[14] However, in 2009, Asians accounted for 40% of all UC undergraduates.[15] And at the premier UC campuses, Asian enrollment is even higher: Asians make up 45.7% of the student population at UC Berkeley;[16] 37.1% at UCLA;[17] 44% at UC San Diego;[18] 52% at UC Irvine;[19] and 30% at UC Davis.[20] This growing imbalance has led the state government to implement new policies intended to balance the demographic breakdown at

---

[13] U.S. Census Bureau. "Resident Population by Race, Hispanic Origin, and State: 2009." *Statistical Abstract of the United States: 2011.* Washington: Government Printing Office, 2010.

[14] *Ibid.*

[15] "Asian-Americans Blast UC Admissions Policy." Associated Press. 24 Apr 2009.

[16] UC Berkeley Planning and Analysis Office. "UC Berkeley Enrollment Data: New Freshman Enrollment by Ethnicity, Fall 2006 through Fall 2010." Web. 15 Feb 2011.

[17] UCLA Department of Student Affairs. "Quick Facts about UCLA." Web. 15 Feb 2011.

[18] UC San Diego. "UC San Diego Facts and Campus Profile." Web. 15 Feb 2011.

[19] UC Irvine. "UCI College Profile." Web. 15 Feb 2011.

[20] UC Davis. "UC Davis Facts: Student Headcount by Ethnicity, Fall 2010." Web. 15 Feb 2011.

the UCs. After all, the UCs are *public* institutions; it makes sense that the state of California would want its schools to better reflect the population of the state as a whole.

There are two key changes that students should be aware of:

1. The SAT Subject Test requirement has been dropped.
2. The Eligibility in the Local Context (ELC) program will be significantly expanded.[21]

Let's see what these changes mean for applicants.

Critics of the SAT Subject Test requirement argued that it left many strong high school seniors—students with high GPAs and SAT scores—ineligible for the UCs. Moreover, too many high school students weren't even aware that the SAT Subject Test was a UC requirement until too late in the game. The UC's own analysis predicts that dropping the SAT Subject Test requirement will most benefit the Caucasian student population, followed by the African-American and Latino populations.[22] Asian-American students, however, have long seen the SAT Subject Tests as a way to highlight their academic achievements and differentiate themselves from other candidates in the admissions process. As the UC notes, there are "stunning differences in test-taking behavior among ethnic groups," which means that only a small number of Asian-American students will benefit from dropping the SAT Subject Test requirement.[23] On the contrary, eliminating this requirement is likely to remove one of the competitive advantages that Asian-American students have long enjoyed.

Introduced in 1999, the Eligibility in the Local Context (ELC) program guarantees a spot at one of the UC campuses to every student ranking in the top 4% of every (participating) California

---

[21] University of California Admissions. "Applying for Fall 2012?" Web. 16 Feb 2011.

[22] University of California Academic Senate. "Eligibility Reform at the University of California and Its Diversity Impact." 22 Jan 2010. Web. 16 Feb 2011.

[23] *Ibid.*

high school class. (Students must also maintain a GPA of 3.0 or higher and complete a specific sequence of UC-mandated coursework.) Starting in 2012, eligibility for the ELC program will be extended to the top 9% of seniors. Now the ELC program is designed to create college opportunities for students from historically underrepresented communities. It ensures that a certain percentage of students from *every* participating California high school can find a place at a UC: whether a student falls in the top 9% at the notoriously competitive and high-achieving Troy High School in Fullerton or at the comparatively easy Santa Ana High School, he or she will be guaranteed a spot at one of the UC campuses. This program clearly helps out students attending weaker high schools. But critics complain that it is not fair to the student who works hard at more competitive schools and does very well, but fails to crack the top 9%.

Instituting these two changes to the UC admissions policy is likely to decrease Asian-American enrollment. As the UC Senate notes, "Asian-Americans are [currently] heavily represented at UC. Opening the door more widely [by changing admissions policies] may reduce their numbers."[24] Understandably, these changes in UC admissions policy have alarmed many Asian-American activist and political groups. Estimates show that the policy change may decrease Asian enrollment across the UC system by nearly 20%.[25] In an open letter, Patrick Hayashi, Associate President of the UC system from 1999 until 2004 and a Japanese American, warns that the new policy "may result in dramatic reductions in minority student admissions at all or

[24] University of California Academic Senate. "Board of Admissions and Relations with Schools: Minutes of Meeting, January 8, 2010." 8 Jan 2010. Web. 16 Feb 2011.

[25] Po, Vivian. "UC Policy Criticized: Change in Admission Rules Could Reduce Number of APAs." *Hokubei Mainichi.* 01 Apr 2009.

nearly all of the [UC] campuses", and said that it "risks sacrificing an entire generation of minority students."[26]

Although these policies continue to be hotly debated, they are currently being implemented. Students should take note and, if necessary, start looking beyond the UC system.

The budget crisis

California's economy has been dealing with some serious budget woes. Because the UC is a public institution supported by the state, the state's problem is also the UC's problem.

One recent proposal recommends that the UC campuses cut the numbers of admitted students. As was reported in a UC newsletter,

> To protect academic excellence and maintain the level of service students expect when they enroll at UC, [this] proposal calls on UC's president to bring enrollments closer to the university's budgeted levels by reducing new freshman enrollment.[27]

In the meantime, however, students are applying in record numbers, not only to the UCs but also to the California State Universities and to community colleges. If the proposal to cut enrollment is accepted and enforced, this will mean that just when more and more students are applying to California state schools, fewer and fewer will be accepted. In other words, UC admission will get exponentially more competitive. So what are California residents to do? This is a question that the state of California has yet to answer.

---

[26] Hayashi, Patrick. "Letter to the Committee on Affirmative Action and Diversity." *APIEL NOW!* Asian and Pacific Islander Education and Languages NOW! 30 Jan 2010. Web. 16 Feb 2011.

[27] UC Davis. "Regents to Consider a Smaller Freshman Class and a Freeze on Senior Management Pay." *Dateline: News for Faculty and Staff.* 09 Jan 2009. Web. 16 Feb 2011.

Tuition increases

Although families in California have historically considered the UCs a more affordable option, this is no longer necessarily the case. Effective January 2010, the UCs raised tuition by over 30%,[28] bringing the cost of attendance for the academic year 2010-2011 to over $30,000.[29] And the increase in tuition has not bought an increase in the quality of education. On the contrary, class sizes are still expanding and the average time to graduation is still unsatisfactory. Currently, only around two out of three UCLA students manage to graduate within four years.[30] Many take up to six years because overcrowding at UCLA prevents students from being able to enroll in classes required for graduation.

All of these developments—the tuition hikes, coupled with admissions policies resulting in a more difficult process for many immigrant families—beg the question: Why apply to a UC? The traditional reasons—lower cost and an easier admission process without sacrifice in quality—are being eroded.

I strongly urge immigrant families to seriously explore their private school options. During this time of uncertainty, it is comforting to know that immigrant students from California are consistently gaining admission to private schools that are ranked higher than the UCs. Students rejected by Berkeley and UCLA are getting admitted to schools such as Johns Hopkins University, the University of Pennsylvania, Dartmouth College, and the University of Chicago. Moreover, parents should know that private colleges, which have more money, are offering attractive financial aid packages to woo qualified students. Families are advised to research their private options thoroughly and expand their horizons.

---

[28] "California: University System moves to Raise Fees." Associated Press. 18 Nov 2009.

[29] UC Berkeley. "Facts at a Glance." Web. 16 Feb 2011.

[30] UCLA Office of Analysis and Information Management. "Data FAQs: Graduation and Retention." Web. 16 Feb 2011.

1.4 Four Common Misconceptions

This book emerged out of a series of articles I wrote for the *Korea Daily*, a Korean-language newspaper published in California. When I first started writing my column, my editors and I suspected that the Korean community was sorely lacking reliable and accurate information about the college admissions process. The response we've received from our readers has overwhelmingly confirmed our suspicions. The immigrant community has been laboring under many widespread but harmful misconceptions about the college admissions process in particular, and the U.S. education system as a whole.

In the rest of this introductory chapter, I introduce four of the most common mistakes that immigrant parents make:

1. Over-emphasizing the importance of the standardized test (usually the SAT).

2. Forcing children to participate in the same activities as everybody else. (Herd mentality)

3. Allowing students free rein over electronic (gaming, computing, communication) devices.

4. Remaining unaware of the full range of college options.

Over-emphasizing the importance of the SAT

Many immigrant parents overestimate the importance of the SAT, believing it to be the most significant factor in the college admissions process. This is very natural, considering the academic culture prevalent in many other countries. In Korea, for example, the college entrance test is offered just once per year, in November of a student's senior year. The entire nation acknowledges the importance of this test: the stock market opens later, traffic—including air traffic—is diverted from testing sites and electric companies stand by in case of power failure. This nationwide obsession is so remarkable that it has been featured in many American newspapers. The *Wall Street Journal*, for example, recently profiled one Korean mother who participated in an overnight prayer session at a temple, bowing three thousand times in order to plead for her son's academic success.[31]

While it is understandable that parents coming from this test culture will have misperceptions about the U.S. education system, parents must realize that the SAT is *not* equivalent to the college entrance test in their home country. It is at once a more forgiving and less significant exam. Unlike other national college entrance exams, the SAT is offered multiple times a year and can be taken during a student's senior, junior or even sophomore years. The test is also much shorter and less comprehensive than other college entrance exams. And most importantly, *it just doesn't count as much*. GPA is the number one factor determining admission at both public and private colleges. SATs come in second: a high SAT score alone will *not* get a student into any competitive college.

Doing the same activities as everyone else (Herd mentality)

In my interactions with the immigrant community, I have found that many students end up with very similar extracurricular résumés. They engage in the same activities as their peers: playing in an orchestra or band, for example, or participating in church activities. Part of this is the natural result of being part of a community. Parents tend to share information about their kids, and kids wants to do what their friends are doing. However, part of this uniformity is caused and nurtured by immigrant culture itself.

Many immigrant cultures tend to value homogeneity. If John's mother sends John to a speech and debate club, Tony's mother feels that she should send Tony as well. In fact, many of the families I counsel seem to think that there is some sort of magic template for getting into college and they come to me to find that secret "formula." They talk about so-and-so, who got into an Ivy

---

[31] Park, SungHa. "On College-Entrance Exam Day, All of South Korea is Put to the Test." *Wall Street Journal*. 12 Nov 2008.

League school by doing A, B, and C, and assume that if their child also does A, B, and C, he or she will also get into an Ivy League school.

This kind of mentality breeds a certain kind of student: the student with good grades and a large number of non-distinctive activities. Most of these students will not get accepted into a top private school. Why? Because the U.S. education system values diversity and rewards individuality. American colleges seek out variety in gender, race, social class, life experience, etc. So they strongly prefer students who distinguish themselves from the pack: students with a unique identity, students who can bring something to the college *that no other student can.*

Granting free access to informational technology

While the over-use of technology is an issue that concerns all teenagers growing up these days, the problem is particularly acute among children of immigrants. A great number of the students I counsel have absolutely no discipline when it comes to using the Internet, playing video games, texting their friends, or participating in other time-consuming electronic gadget-driven activities. Parents feel that there is nothing that they can do to solve this problem. However, this is not true.

Initially, as a college counselor, I didn't think that my job required me to get involved in matters like this. But the problem is too common and widespread for me to pass over without mention. Too many students suffer academically because of their inability to manage time. And when a student cannot maintain his or her academic performance because of an addiction to some form of technology, it is the parents' job to cut off access.

Remaining unaware of the full array of college options

Although the immigrant community in the U.S. has become better informed and organized over the last few decades, immigrants still remain largely unaware of the vast academic opportunities available to them. Students tend to apply to the same ten or twelve schools, thinking that admission into these institutions guarantees long-term success. Again, this notion can be traced back to realities in home countries, where greater emphasis is placed on college affiliation.

Just consider, however, the following piece of information. Among the top twenty-five schools in the U.S. there are many colleges that the average immigrant parent will never have heard of. Schools like Rice, Northwestern, Emory, and Vanderbilt all rank above UC Berkeley, but Berkeley sits on the top of many an immigrant parent's college wish-list.[32] Students of immigrant families are limiting their options because of a simple lack of information, and in the current ultra-competitive college environment, they are doing themselves a real disservice.

*　　*　　*

In the following chapters, I will discuss these misconceptions in greater detail and seek to replace them with accurate information about the U.S. admissions process. I will also present and analyze several real-life case studies to help illustrate central points, introducing readers to some less familiar colleges along the way.

Many immigrant parents come to America at great personal cost in order to ensure a better future for their children. It is our hope that this book will help them realize their dreams—that it will show them how to take maximal advantage of the wonderful educational opportunities that their sacrifice has made available to their children.

---

[32] "National University Rankings 2011." *U.S. News & World Report.* 17 Aug 2010.

Chapter 2:
GPA and Course Selection

The college admissions process has become increasingly competitive. It seems that students these days must excel in all areas: they must be straight-A students, stellar test-takers and motivated leaders in the community. Now this picture isn't entirely factual. There is definitely room within the American higher education system for students who are less than outstanding in one or more areas of the college admissions process.

However, one section of the application does demand a strong performance: the high school transcript. Remember, this is the number one factor in college admissions! And the transcript is not just a list of numbers and grades. It is a far more revealing document: one that illustrates the choices a student has made, his or her perseverance, intellectual interests, and academic successes.

In this chapter, I'll explain how colleges evaluate GPA. Then I'll answer three of the questions I most frequently get asked on this topic. I'll give case studies of two very different students in order to show what effect their GPA had on their college prospects. Finally, in the last section, I'll discuss the International Baccalaureate (IB) option and compare it with the AP system, which is much more common in the U.S.

2.1 How Colleges Evaluate GPA

The high school GPA is the most important factor for admissions at virtually every college in the U.S. However, many students don't understand exactly how colleges evaluate high school transcripts. This lack of information often causes students to make decisions that ultimately jeopardize rather than boost their chances of admissions success. In this section, I'll share some insights, gleaned from looking at thousands of high school transcripts, into how private and public schools "read" this important document and evaluate the information provided in it.

Calculating GPA

At the most basic level, GPA is just the mathematical average of all grades attained in high school. The simplicity of this definition is, however, deeply deceptive. In actual practice, a student's GPA is not a fixed number! In fact, the number on display on the high school transcript may well be different from the number that actually gets reviewed by colleges.

First of all, different colleges consider different subsections of the transcript as part of their evaluation process. Some schools, including Stanford and the UCs, consider coursework only from sophomore year on. Others schools, such as the University of Southern California (USC), consider coursework from 9th through 11th grade—but also request senior-year, fall-term grades. (In fact, almost all colleges require a senior fall mid-term grade report.)

Second of all, different colleges follow different weighting rubrics. In fact, many high schools have different weighting policies, too. The "weighted" GPA is a calculation of GPA that adds extra value to grades achieved in classes characterized as honors, accelerated, AP or IB. For example, some high schools might tack on a half-letter to grades attained in AP classes. According to this weighting principle, getting a B in an AP course would be roughly equivalent to getting an A– in a non-honors course. However, some high schools don't weight grades at all. In order to equalize the playing field, each college uses its own weighting system to recalculate students' GPA.

The UCs, like some other state systems but unlike private schools, have a well-publicized minimum GPA requirement and weighting formula. In order to get admitted, California residents must have a minimum 3.0 weighted high school GPA (out-of-state students need a GPA of 3.4 or above). GPA is calculated using only grades received in "a-g" courses—a list of fifteen year-long mandatory courses taken in 10th and 11th grade—with extra points given for up to eight semesters of honors-level coursework.[33]

Though the UCs are open about their admission standards, private colleges are generally not. In fact, the weighting formulae and the "cut-off GPAs" of private colleges remain highly privileged information. So how can students know whether they're doing what they have to do to get into these private colleges? And what can they do to make themselves more attractive?

What students should do

Although students don't have access to specific numerical standards and secret GPA-calculating algorithms, they still know all they need to know. *All* colleges, whatever their specific weighting system, are looking for something called "strength of curriculum." They want to reward students who take—and succeed in—the most challenging courses available to them. Stanford University, for example, clearly announces its philosophy on this matter. On its admissions page, it says, "We want to see that [students] have challenged [themselves] by taking some of the accelerated, honors, Advanced Placement, or International Baccalaureate courses, if they are offered."[34] To put

---

[33] University of California Admissions. "California Residents." Web. 16 Feb 2011.

[34] Stanford University Undergraduate Admission. "School Reports and Transcripts." Web. 16 Feb 2011.

it simply, the students who succeed at competitive colleges are the students who succeeded in the most challenging courses available to them in their high schools.

However, the high school transcript speaks to more than just academic performance. It also tells a surprisingly detailed story about a student's intellectual character and development. Attractive candidates demonstrate intellectual fearless-ness by taking the most rigorous courses on offer. They don't back off after a first B but rather renew their determination go succeed. Students who shy away from such challenges appear to lack the motivation, ability or courage necessary to flourish in a highly competitive intellectual environment.

But what about students who don't have access to a whole bunch of advanced courses? Let's look again at what Stanford says. Its admissions officers are looking for students who have taken challenging courses "*if they are offered.*" Students can only take advantage of opportunities that are available to them. Therefore, students attending schools that do not offer the full range of AP classes or, say, the IB diploma option (see below) shouldn't worry: they will not be penalized for this in the admissions process. However, universities are impressed by students who go above and beyond the norm and create opportunities for themselves. If a course isn't being offered in a student's high school, he or she can consider taking an equivalent class at a nearby accredited college or university.

This is also a worthwhile endeavor if a student would like to explore a subject matter in greater depth or at a more advanced level. Seeking out advanced studies is a great way to show initiative, develop specific intellectual passions, and demonstrate a genuine love of learning. In fact, the University of Pennsylvania emphasizes this point. On its admissions website, it says, "We pay close attention to the types and levels of courses taken and the grades achieved, *particularly as they relate to [students'] educational interests.*"[35] So students applying to study international relations, for example, might want to take a second foreign language at their local community college. Or students intending to be engineering majors might want to take some college-level science courses.

(On a side note, students might be able to gain college credit for college-level coursework completed in high school. Every school has its own policy, however. The University of Pennsylvania, for example, has an unusually easygoing approach: it gives credit for all coursework undertaken on a college campus so long as the course is part of the normal college curriculum and is published in the college catalog. Not all colleges will be as accepting about transfer credits.)

To summarize, students should remember that the high school transcript—grades, weighted by the strength of the curriculum taken—is the single most important factor in college admissions. No SAT (or ACT) score and no extracurricular activity can compensate for a poor GPA or a weak academic course load. And there are no shortcuts! Some students inevitably try to "game" the system and raise their GPA the easy way. The next section should serve as due warning to any such students reading this.

"Faking it": What not to do

Some students try to take "easy" courses, figuring that the "easy A" they receive in a class like ceramics will boost their overall GPA. However, classes are *not* created equal! Colleges place the greatest emphasis on grades received in core academic subjects: math, English, social studies, science, and foreign language. So the A earned in ceramics is definitely not equivalent to the A received in AP U.S. History! Many schools don't even factor such grades in when they calculate GPA.

---

[35] Penn Admissions. "High School Preparation." Web. 16 Feb 2011.

Other students decide to take a "regular" class instead of an AP class, again trying to take the easy way out. However, an A received in regular U.S. History is not equivalent to an A—or even a B—earned in AP U.S. History. Remember: colleges factor grades against the difficulty of the coursework to assess how much of an achievement the grade really is.

Some students get even craftier. They take classes that they're worried about over the summer at a community college. Or they choose to take Chinese as their foreign language when they're native Chinese speakers. Students have been warned: these tricks are transparent. Admissions officers have seen them all before, and they're not going to fall for them.

2.2 Frequently Asked Questions about GPA

The last section offered some general advice and information about the GPA. This section answers three specific, frequently asked questions:

1. Which classes should I take?

2. How much does it matter that my grades go up and down?

3. Can I get a C and still get into one of the most selective schools?

Which classes should I take?

The simple answer is: take the most challenging courses available while leaving time to "have a life," pursue passion projects and develop extracurricular activities.

More specifically, though, students should make sure to take *four years* of coursework in the core academic subjects: math, English, social studies, science, and foreign language. Why is this important?

I'll illustrate this through a case study. Fred has taken three years of high school French and doesn't much feel like taking AP

French his senior year. He's heard it's a hard class…and French was never his strong suit. And anyway, Fred wants to be an engineer! What should Fred do?

Well, let's look at this from the college admissions officer's perspective. The high school transcript can be seen as a "predictor." In other words, it demonstrates how a student might be expected to perform at the college level. Now the easiest class at a top-tier college will be harder than the hardest class in high school. If Fred is worried about managing the most challenging coursework at his high school, then colleges will be appropriately concerned about his ability to perform at their schools. Furthermore, colleges like students to show a certain baseline interest in becoming a well-informed, conversant citizen of the world. This might sound vague, even hokey, but there's a reason why colleges maintain a distribution requirement that forces math majors to take foreign languages and music majors to take introductory science classes! This brings us to one last reason Fred should take AP French—and as many other AP classes as he can. Many colleges give students the chance to "opt out" of certain distribution requirements if they attain qualifying AP scores (generally 3 or 4 and above). If Fred doesn't take AP French his senior year, chances are he'll have to take its equivalent as a freshman in college!

Of course, realistically, there might be times when scheduling conflicts prohibit a student from taking certain classes. Maybe AP French and AP Calculus are scheduled at the same time. As a student interested in majoring in engineering, Fred should by all means take AP Calculus and forego AP French. However, the scheduling conflict should be addressed in Fred's application, preferably by his school counselor. Fred could also overcome this conflict by taking French at a community college. This would show initiative as well as dedication to really mastering French.

Let's look at two more case studies, focusing now specifically on the choice of AP courses. Many students are unsure of which AP classes they should take and how many they should take in a given year or semester. Such decisions become especially difficult when scheduling conflicts occur.

Stephanie is currently a sophomore at a competitive public school in the Bay Area. She has managed to get mostly As, though also a handful of Bs, in her first three semesters of high school and she expects to maintain a similar GPA this semester. Stephanie must now register for her junior-year classes. She is committed to taking Spanish 3, Precalculus, English 3, and AP Chemistry. But she is undecided about AP U.S. History: she has heard lots of horror stories about the difficulty of the class and the massive amounts of work involved. In fact, many of her upperclassmen friends have discouraged her from taking the course. But Stephanie has also heard that colleges prefer students who take challenging courses. With so many conflicting pieces of advice, Stephanie isn't sure how to proceed. How much would the decision *not* to take the AP course affect her admissions prospects? Should she take AP U.S. History?

Now before we try to answer this question, we need more information about Stephanie's college goals. There are rarely simple and universal yes-or-no answers to any admissions question. All students are different, and their decisions should be informed by their specific goals.

We have to factor in, for example, the fact that Stephanie is targeting the top-ranked schools in the UC system (UCLA, UC Berkeley) as well as a few selective private colleges. This means that her competition will most likely be taking—and acing—AP U.S. History. We also need to weigh in what we know about Stephanie's abilities and her work ethic. Stephanie has maintained a strong GPA so far. Her academic history suggests not only that she has the ability to do well in AP U.S. History, but also that it would be only natural for her to seek out maximally challenging courses as a junior. So even though the thought of tacking on AP U.S. History to an already packed course load is daunting to Stephanie, I would recommend that she sign up for the course. AP U.S. History will provide Stephanie with a chance to demonstrate her academic prowess. And taking the class will show that Stephanie is not the kind of student who shies away from a challenge. Of course, my recommendation assumes that Stephanie would put in a real effort.

Let's look at a rather different case. Michael, a freshman, loves learning languages. A Japanese-American with a fairly good grasp of his mother tongue, Michael developed an interest in foreign languages from an early age. He completed Spanish 1 in junior high school and is currently enrolled in Spanish 2, with stellar results. Michael is also studying Chinese on his own. His parents are aware of his talent and would like to see him develop his potential in this area. Their question is, How can Michael best develop and demonstrate this genuine passion for languages to colleges?

I had three specific recommendations for Michael.

- Michael should continue taking Spanish through the AP level, making sure to continue to achieve high grades. This would demonstrate consistency and a commitment to fully mastering the language.

- Michael should also take the Japanese SAT, aiming for a perfect score. This would allow Michael to demonstrate his Japanese language skills, something which colleges would not otherwise be aware of.

- Finally, Michael should continue studying Chinese on his own—since he does not have space to add it to his school schedule—with the goal of eventually sitting the AP Chinese Language and Culture Exam. A high score on this test would enable Michael to prove that his self-study was highly effective—just as effective, in fact, as studying Chinese in school over a period of years would have been.

Following these recommendations and attaining the above goals would certainly result in a college application that spotlights Michael's passion and gift for learning languages. And if Michael develops an interest in certain related majors, such as international relations or political science, he would have a definite advantage over other applicants with similar grades in similar classes but no cohesive and demonstrable intellectual interests.

Does it matter that my grades have fluctuated?

Students who are competitive at the most selective colleges generally have consistently strong grades across the board. This means that the simple and blunt answer to the above question is, Yes.

However, a more detailed answer to this question would have to take into consideration the particular kind of fluctuation evident in the transcript. For example, junior- and senior-year courses are generally more advanced and more difficult than freshman- and sophomore-year courses. Because the courses get harder, grades received during junior and senior year mean more: they demonstrate a student's ability to succeed when confronted with advanced material. This means that a weak freshman year can be compensated for, though not canceled out, by strong junior-year grades in suitably more advanced courses. It also means that even an impeccable freshman year can't make up for a disastrous junior year, no matter how aggressive the freshman-year coursework.

Second-semester grades are slightly more important than first-semester grades for the same reason: coursework tends to get more difficult as the year progresses. Therefore, the student who gets a B in AP Chemistry the first semester of junior year but improves to an A the second semester is in a better position than the student who starts off with an A but then slides down to a B.

It is important to understand, however, that a steadily improving GPA is absolutely meaningless if the higher grades are attained only by scaling back on coursework, whether by taking fewer courses or by dialing back the difficulty level. Again, college admissions officers have seen every trick in the book when it comes to trying to make a high school transcript seem better than it really is. But when it comes to this part of the college application, nothing but hard work and consistent accomplishment will look like hard work and consistent accomplishment.

Can I get a C and still get into one of the most selective colleges?

I referred this question to a member of FLEX's InfoBank™, a former Admissions Representative at both Stanford University and a top-ten liberal arts college. The short answer to this question? No: a student who gets a C cannot get into one of the most selective private schools.

Now there may have been very good reasons for the C. Maybe the student is brilliant at math and science but just not that good at the humanities. Maybe the student was too busy studying for the SATs and the APs and participating in various extracurricular activities to find time to ace that one tricky class. These are reasonable explanations. However, the most selective private colleges get so many applications from students with perfect or near-perfect GPAs that they simply don't need to select a student with a less stellar academic record.

The good news is that there *is* still room at lots of excellent colleges for such a student. Additionally, if the C is a one-off anomaly caused by some personal circumstance legitimately beyond the student's control—a serious illness or a family trauma, for example—then the student can explain the situation. (Usually, the school guidance counselor is the best person to provide this information. For this and lots of other reasons, it is a very good idea for students to get to know their guidance counselors...and to make sure their guidance counselors get to know them! A guidance counselor can be an invaluable help in the college admissions process.)

*   *   *

By the end of the first semester of senior year, every student has a long record of the academic choices made and the scholarly successes attained over the last three and a half years. The high school GPA is one area of the college admissions process that just requires good old-fashioned hard work. There are no "tricks" or "gimmicks" to be used here. So the only advice I can give is: take the hardest courses available and excel at them! Though this may sound heartless to students struggling right now to juggle a heavy course load, this is the reality of college admissions today.

Remember the illustration given in chapter one of the college selection process by the Stanford admissions officer. Think of all 30,000+ applications received at schools like Stanford, piled up all over the admissions office floor. Remember that of all these applications, only those that are deemed academically qualified will get on the table for serious consideration. What exactly gets these roughly 21,000 applications off the floor? Academics. GPA and SAT (or ACT) scores. These numbers are *decisive* in getting applications past the first cut. But once applications are on the table, academic achievements no longer play a decisive role. Schools don't rank students in order of SAT score or cumulative GPA and then start admitting students from the top down. No: at this stage, admissions officers want to get to know each applicant's individual story as revealed through his or her extracurricular activities, essays and recommendations. In other words, in most cases GPA is just an initial qualifier and not the final deciding factor. Still, GPA is of crucial importance, and for most students, it should be their highest priority. Although a great GPA won't be enough to get a student in—and a perfect GPA is never absolutely required—a low GPA is enough to get a student rejected.

2.3 Case Study:
Dan, the Good but Not Perfect Student

We will now turn to consider the profile of a student whose GPA put him "on the table" at top-tier private schools. Now realistically, to get into a school such as Harvard or Stanford, a student must do everything right. Students who get into these schools take the most challenging course loads (5 APs senior and often junior year) and still make straight As. However, as the profile below will illustrate, students need not be *perfect* to have a realistic shot at many of the most selective colleges, including some Ivy League schools.

Dan came to us with a strong but far from perfect transcript. This is what Dan's sophomore-year transcript looked like:

Course	Fall Semester	Spring Semester
Honors Algebra 2/Trigonometry	B+	A
Honors Chemistry	B	A-
English	A	A
World History and Government	A	A
Spanish	A	A
PE	A	A
Orchestra	A	A

This is the academic record of a student with strengths in the humanities but some difficulties with math and science. Notice that Dan did *not* receive straight As; however, he also didn't get anything lower than a B. In addition, he was able to pull each of his Bs up to an A during the second semester, which is important because, as colleges well know, second-semester coursework tends to be more difficult than first-semester coursework.

In the summer after his sophomore year, Dan traveled to the East Coast and attended the summer program at Columbia University. He took a course in Constitutional Law and left with an A.

Let's see how things went Dan's junior year:

Course	Fall Semester	Spring Semester
Precalculus	A	A−
AP Statistics	B	B+
AP Biology	B−	B+
Honors English	A+	A
U.S. History	A−	A−
Spanish	A−	A
Orchestra	A	A

Notice that Dan dropped from honors to regular math. Normally, this would raise a red flag, especially since math was Dan's weak point, but he compensated for this by doubling up on math, taking AP Statistics. This demonstrated that Dan was not just taking the easy way out.

Science was also not an area of strength for Dan, but he continued to challenge himself by taking AP Biology. He began that class with a B− but was able to raise his grade to a B+ during that crucial second semester. A private school admissions officer would certainly see and appreciate the effort and character demonstrated by this course selection and performance.

Moreover, Dan's transcript continued to shine in his areas of strength. He pulled excellent grades across the humanities: in English, U.S. History and Spanish.

In the summer after his junior year, Dan took one course at a local community college—Introduction to Biotechnology—and again earned a solid A. Dan's decision to spend two summers in a row taking courses in subjects not available at his public high school was revelatory of Dan's intellectual curiosity. Obviously, Dan didn't take these courses to get a head start on schoolwork. And the high grades that Dan earned demonstrated that he took these courses seriously and applied himself, even though these grades wouldn't factor into his GPA. This was a great testament to Dan's integrity.

Now let's look at Dan's senior-year courses and his Fall semester grades—the last grades that colleges saw when considering Dan's application for admission:

Course	Fall Semester
AP Calculus AB	B
Honors Physics	A-
AP English	A
Economics	A
AP Spanish	A-
Orchestra	A

In his all-important senior year, Dan continued to demonstrate the willingness to face challenges in math and science. He dropped from an AP science to an honors science but didn't drop the sciences altogether, instead completing a full four years of science. And although he didn't take Honors Precalculus his junior year, he chose to take AP Calculus AB his senior year. His junior-year math coursework prevented him from taking AP Calculus BC, but admissions officers would have applauded Dan's decision to take a fourth year of math. Dan also finished a full four years in English, social studies and foreign language. Although he didn't end up with any AP-level coursework in social studies, he did take at least one AP in every other major subject area (math, science, English and Spanish). He fully demonstrated to colleges both the willingness to try, and the ability to succeed in, difficult courses. Colleges could reasonably expect that Dan would continue to demonstrate the same level of academic initiative and accomplishment in college.

Dan's transcript painted the picture of an academically curious student: not a perfect student, but one who was willing to work hard and seek out challenges. Dan was a student who got the balance right. Armed with a good SAT score, great extracurricular activities, well-crafted essays and glowing recommendations, Dan had a shot at several of the top-tier universities, including Brown, Cornell, Dartmouth, Johns

Hopkins, and Northwestern. Of course, nobody could *guarantee* that Dan would get into any one of these schools. And as I have to emphasize, Dan only had a realistic shot at these schools because his good-but-not-perfect transcript was accompanied by uniformly and uncommonly strong performances in all the other areas of his application.

At the end of the day, Dan gained admission to Brown, Dartmouth, Johns Hopkins, and Tufts University. He was rejected from Columbia, Cornell, Georgetown, and U Penn.

Prospective applicants should take home the following moral from this case study. The perfect GPA is not the end-all, be-all of the college admissions process. A 4.0 alone won't get students in. Of course a GPA that is too low will get a student rejected— but a less than perfect GPA need not foreclose on Ivy hopes.

2.4 Case Study: Debbie, the Struggling Student

Let's turn now to a very different case study. Debbie was an average happy-go-lucky teenager at La Cañada High School. She was not particularly academically inclined and didn't really like school; she was much more enthusiastic about surfing the Internet and texting with her friends. To no surprise, her high school transcript wasn't in the best shape. Many readers will know a student like Debbie. Whether for lack of motivation or academic aptitude, she found herself with some poor grades at the end of her sophomore year, when I first met her. At that point, Debbie was just hoping to get into a good UC. My job was to help her maximize her chances of getting into a UC like Irvine, Davis, or Santa Barbara.

This is what Debbie's sophomore-year transcript looked like:

Course	Fall Semester	Spring Semester
Honors Algebra 2/Trigonometry	B+	B+
Chemistry	B	B
Spanish 2	B	B-
English	C+	C
World History	C+	C+
Art	A	B+
PE	A	A

Debbie's unweighted GPA was a 2.93. Currently, a weighted GPA of 3.5 is only good enough to get into UC Santa Cruz and UC Riverside—and a 3.0 is the minimum needed to apply.

Let's first calculate Debbie's weighted GPA. Remember that different colleges have different ways of calculating GPA, and that the UCs—unlike private colleges—are very open about the details. We know exactly how the UCs weight GPA and exactly what the GPA cut-off is (3.0, weighted, for California residents). In particular, we know that:

- GPA is calculated using only grades achieved in the "a-g" UC-mandated subjects.

- A maximum of eight AP or UC-approved honors courses are weighted.

- Grades do not come in pluses or minuses. For example, a B+ and a B– both count as a B.

Now let's apply this information to Debbie's transcript.

Debbie took one advanced course in 10th grade—Honors Algebra 2/Trigonometry—and received a creditable B+. However, the UCs do not award honor or AP credit for Honors Algebra 2/Trigonometry at La Cañada High. (Students can check whether specific courses at their high school receive the weighting credit by looking up their high schools on the UC website.) As a result, Debbie might as well have taken a regular class and received an A. Additionally, Debbie received Cs in English and World History, putting her cumulative sophomore-year GPA at *under* 3.0. In other words, as a sophomore, Debbie did not meet the minimum requirement for UC eligibility.

For Debbie, everything rested on her junior-year course selection and GPA. Schoolwork had to take top priority, even at the expense of developing her extracurricular profile. Unless Debbie raised her GPA, she wouldn't even have the *option* of applying to a UC. So for Debbie, it was very important for her to pick junior-year courses that would maximize her chances of academic success.

Students like Debbie are often better served by taking regular classes than by struggling through APs. Although we encourage students to take the most rigorous courses they can handle, a C doesn't count as "handling" a course. Bluntly, students should not take an AP or honors class at the expense of getting a C! With this in mind, here is the course schedule we recommended for Debbie's junior year:

- Precalculus (regular or honors)
- Physics (regular)
- U.S. History (regular)
- English (regular)
- Spanish 3 (regular), and
- an elective: Drama (or some other elective that would satisfy the "Visual and Performing Arts" requirement).

With the possible exception of math, we encouraged Debbie to stick with regular classes, making sure she got As and Bs in all her classes. Debbie could have elected to take either regular or honors Precalculus (she would receive an honors credit for the advanced class), because her comparatively strong performance in math her sophomore year suggested she was capable of succeeding on the honors math track. However, we recommended that Debbie *not* take honors-level options in her humanities classes, since she evidently had weaknesses in those areas and coursework would only get harder her junior year. Finally, we recommended that Debbie take an elective class, such as drama, that would enable her to do something she enjoyed while earning a relatively easy A.

Now the recommendations above were targeted at a very specific student. We counseled Debbie on the assumption that the general level of motivation and academic achievement she had demonstrated so far was indicative of what was to come. If Debbie were willing and eager to make some drastic change in attitude or in her approach to her studies, our counsel could have been different.

This is where parents play a vital role in the college planning process. Parental involvement is a not-often-discussed but crucial part of the college admissions process. That is why in the FLEX college counseling program, we meet with the *entire* family whenever possible in order to gain a comprehensive assessment of each student and his or her support system.

Let's say that Debbie, faced with the sobering reality of her academic prospects, decided that she would put in a tremendous effort her upcoming junior year. Let's further say that Debbie's parents, with a *realistic* assessment of Debbie's character and aptitude, trusted Debbie to really see this change of heart through. In this case, we might have recommended that Debbie take a challenging course such as AP Statistics to give her academic record a real jolt. However, such a move would have been obviously risky: if it turned out that she were actually unable or unwilling to do the work necessary to succeed in AP Statistics, she could have forfeited any chance of getting into a UC.

Now as a college counselor, I certainly don't want to tell other parents how to do their job. First of all, I know it is all too easy for a third party to make recommendations. It's the students and parents who have to do all the hard work! And second of all, as a parent myself, I don't think other people should tell me how to be a parent! Nevertheless, parental involvement can seriously affect a student's academic success, and I know from experience that even well-meaning and genuinely concerned parents can still have serious blindspots.

Take Debbie, for example. Debbie's parents granted Debbie complete freedom to surf the Internet and rack up minutes on her cell phone. It's a parent's job to monitor the use of such technology—and to enforce a blackout when necessary. (Contrary to what teenagers would have parents believe, students do *not* need constant access to the Internet to get their schoolwork done.) For Debbie to have a realistic shot at securing UC eligibility, her parents needed to be more involved. They needed to have an accurate understanding about their child's personality and her capacities, both intellectually and temperamentally. And they needed to be willing to force her to eliminate temptations and distraction. Debbie and her family needed to make some cold and unemotional decisions in light of her sophomore-year record. The good news, though, was that Debbie still had the time to decisively alter her college prospects. Everything depended on her performance her junior year.

As it turned out, Debbie was able to find the necessary focus her junior year. She followed our advice regarding her junior-year course selection and focused all her attention on her school grades, dropping her flute lessons and scaling back some of her commitments to her church youth group praise team. With the extra time—and with a lot more parental vigilance—she was able to bring her grades up and eventually secured admission to UC Irvine, UC Davis and Boston University.

2.5 The International Baccalaureate (IB) Program

In this last section of chapter two, I'll introduce students to the International Baccalaureate (IB) program. In many ways, IB coursework is similar to Advanced Placement (AP) course-work. Both programs have similar strengths and weaknesses. At their best, IB and AP courses both challenge students to master advanced material and to develop sophisticated study skills and habits that will be invaluable to them as college students. But both programs also face the same criticism: as with all programs culminating in a standardized test, the IB and AP have been said to limit creativity and force teachers to "teach to the test."

There are, of course, major differences between the IB and AP programs. First of all, the IB program is significantly less widespread and well-known in the U.S. While 34% of American public high schools offer AP courses in the core subject areas (English, math, science, and social studies), only 2.8% offer the IB Diploma.[36] One consequence of this is that fewer colleges offer college credit for IB coursework than for AP coursework.

Secondly, although IB courses, like AP classes, are highly demanding college-level courses culminating in standardized examinations, students in the IB stream have the further option of taking the entire IB curriculum: a sweeping two-year program that results in a special IB diploma. Requirements include a course called "The Theory of Knowledge," an extensive 4,000-word research paper and 150 hours of community service. IB diploma candidates are also required to pass six IB exams (three standard exams and three advanced exams) in the six core subject groups: language, second language, social science, math and computer science, experimental science, and the arts.

One demerit of the IB system is that there is very little flexibility built into the program. Because of the regimented set of requirements and coursework, the IB program—compared to the AP option—leaves little room for students to take initiative or explore their academic preferences.

On the other hand, one advantage the IB system enjoys over the AP track in that it is a thoughtfully constructed full curriculum, not an a la carte menu of course options. Courses are designed to function in a complementary way to give the student a solid

---

[36] College Board Advocacy and Policy Center. "Percentage of Public High Schools Offering Core AP® or IB Courses in the Four Core Subject Area." Web. 16 Feb 2011.

grounding in a wide variety of subjects. Additionally, the extra-academic features of the IB, such as the community service requirement, force students to develop qualities they might not exercise in the classroom. Few students would be disciplined enough to engage in 150 hours of community service on their own! These stringent requirements, in combination with the limited availability of the IB diploma in American high schools, can give the IB an aura of "prestige" or exclusivity.

How should we weigh the advantages and disadvantages of the IB system against those of the AP track? How does a college admissions officer view the two programs? Is one better received than the other? And should parents and students seek out one program over the other?

When a college admissions office says that its officers evaluate an applicant based on the curricular opportunities available at the applicant's own high school, it's telling the truth. The good news for students and parents is that admissions officers do not favor IB over AP or vice versa. During this time of hyper-competitive college admissions, families should not bring additional stress on themselves by *seeking out* an IB high school when their local high school already offers a strong selection of AP courses. What is important is that a student take advantage of the most demanding courses available to him or her. Doing so will give colleges all the evidence they need that the student is capable of performing at the collegiate level. (Of course, each student must find the right balance between taking advanced college-level courses and earning high grades: as we already emphasized, taking AP or IB courses and earning Cs is definitely worse than taking "regular" courses and earning As.) An Associate Director of Admissions at Cornell University summarized the moral of the story the best. "No matter which program your school offers," she advised, "challenge yourself! We want to see that you took advantage of some challenging opportunities at your school. AP and IB both fit into this category."[37]

But let's get a bit more specific. What should a student do if his or her high school offers *both* IB and AP courses? Which track should the student take? To better weigh this matter, let's consider the following case study.

Alice was a high school student who wanted to double up on her sciences in the next school year. To do so would have required her to leave the IB track she was on, since it did not offer her the flexibility to take two science classes in one year. However, she was concerned that such a change would reflect poorly on her when applying to colleges. What should Alice do?

To answer this question, let's consider what kind of student benefits most from taking the IB curriculum. The ideal IB student is a gifted individual who thrives under the challenge of advanced coursework, but does not have a focused academic interest yet. This student prefers to get a broad education covering the humanities, science, and math without concentrating on any particular area. Now the truth is that many high school and even lots of college students fall under this category. It takes a while to identify the field where talents and interests best line up. In fact, most colleges don't allow freshmen to declare their majors, preferring to allow students up to two years of freedom to explore several interests and seek out their real calling.

But of course there are other kinds of students. Some students have longstanding and very specific interests. Alice, for instance, had always been very interested in the natural sciences and she wanted to take full advantage of the range of AP courses and electives her high school had to offer within this particular genre. Other students might realize that they are very passionate about a subject matter that is not featured within the IB curriculum,

---

[37] Cornell engineering Office of Admission. "IB vs. AP." *Cornell engineering Admissions Blog.* 08 Feb 2007. Web. 16 Feb 2011.

which the strictures of the diploma program would not allow them to explore. For such students, taking AP courses might very well be the better way to go. AP courses provide students with greater freedom and flexibility in customizing their high school education. So we recommended that Alice leave the IB track and pursue her passion.

As always, there are no cookie-cutter answers to admissions questions. As with all aspects of education, each student must figure out what is in his or her best interest. With regard to the IB and AP programs, the most we can say is that when given the choice between the two systems, students who have a clear sense of where their talents and interests lie should take advantage of the freedom given them to design their own AP curricula, whereas students who are less sure of their direction should undertake the broad and general education provided for by the IB curriculum. With this information in hand, students should make an educated decision as to what will be best for them, remembering above all that—as I have emphasized throughout this chapter—receiving excellent grades in demanding courses takes top priority.

Chapter 3:
The SATs and the ACT

Every year, over two million high school students take the SAT.[38] The very mention of this test often causes great anxiety; in fact, studying for the SAT has become a rite of passage, with parents signing their children up for test prep courses as early as 7th grade. This focus on test preparation is partly justified. After GPA, the SAT score—or the ACT score—is the most important factor in college admissions. However, parents all too often over-emphasize the importance of the SAT score at the expense of other admissions factors.

In this chapter, I'll explain the nature and purpose of the SAT and provide some general tips on how to prepare for the test. I'll also discuss the role that SAT scores play in getting into the most selective colleges—schools like Harvard and Stanford—and then the somewhat different role that SAT scores play in getting into other private schools and public schools.

Of course, the SAT isn't the only game in town. The ACT is gaining on the SAT in popularity and prominence, and it is now an equally good option for students to consider. Wherever the SAT is accepted, the ACT is also accepted. So this chapter also

---

[38] College Board. "Why Take the SAT." Web. 17 Feb 2011.

compares the two standardized tests and offers students some guidelines for focusing on one or the other.

After discussing the SAT and the ACT, I'll turn to the SAT Subject Tests. These tests are the least important components of a student's academic profile. However, for some schools and some majors, the SAT Subject Tests are still extremely important and should take high priority. Other students, however, will not need to take any SAT Subject Tests. I'll give readers some idea of the range of SAT Subject Test policies out there and offer guidelines for deciding which tests to take.

3.1 The SAT

Although the SAT gets a lot of attention and everyone has heard a great deal about it, in my experience, I've discovered that too many students and their parents fundamentally misunderstand the nature of the test. So let's start with some basics:

1. What does the SAT look like?
2. What does it test for?
3. Why do colleges require it?

What does the SAT look like?

Let's get some basic information about the SAT out of the way. As most students will already know, the SAT tests abilities in three subjects: Critical Reading, Math and Writing. Altogether, the SAT is three hours and forty-five minutes long. This includes nine scored sections: three Writing sections (one essay plus two multiple-choice grammar sections), three Critical Reading sections and three Math sections.

Part	Subject	Time
1	One Writing section (essay)	25 min
2-6	Two Critical Reading sections	25 min each
	Two Math sections	25 min each
	One Writing section (grammar)	25 min
7-8	One Critical Reading section	20 min
	One Math section	20 min
9	One Writing section (grammar)	10 min

There is also a tenth section, also twenty-five minutes long, that does not count toward the student's score. This is the experimental section. It may test Critical Reading, Writing or Math; there is no way to know what kind of experimental section a student will get and there is no way to identify for sure which section is the experimental section.

What does the SAT test for?

In the words of the College Board, the organization that writes and administers the SAT, "The SAT...tests the *skills* you're learning in school: reading, writing and math. Your knowledge and skills in these subjects are important for success in college and throughout your life."[39] In other words, the SAT isn't designed to test knowledge or retention of concepts learned in school. It's designed to test the ability to think critically, reason things out, and solve puzzles—*skills* that are supposed to get trained and developed in school no matter what the student is learning.

---

[39] College Board. "What is the SAT?" Web. 17 Feb 2011.

Why do many colleges require the SAT?

In assessing general *skills* rather than *knowledge retention,* the SAT is designed to level the playing field and provide colleges with a piece of quantified, easily comparable data that can be used to identify the "best" students.

How does the SAT level the playing field? Consider two students from very different high schools. One attends a Midwestern public high school which offers very few AP courses. Another attends Stuyvesant, a high-prestige public high school in New York City. Both students maintain straight As in their coursework…but the student from New York City has taken more difficult courses and has had the opportunity to participate in summer research internships. How could a college measure these two students against each other? The SAT can help students who haven't had the same opportunities shine and compete with their better situated peers. An excellent SAT score will identify the Midwestern student as someone who most likely would have thrived in the more intense New York school system. That is, the SAT helps colleges compensate for differences in opportunities.

Of course, the SAT doesn't simply favor students from less competitive high schools. Consider two further students, again from very different high schools, applying to the same college. One student has a 3.9 GPA from Harvard-Westlake, one of the premier private high schools in the U.S. The other has a 4.4 at a public high school in Southern California with a far less rigorous curriculum. How is a college admissions officer supposed to compare these two students? Is it fair to say that the student with the lower GPA is less academically able? Again, this is where the SAT comes into play. Since all students across the nation— and increasingly in other countries—take the same test, colleges can compare their academic abilities.

Although, as we saw in chapter one, college admissions officers are giving less weight to the SAT and putting more emphasis on GPA, the SAT is obviously still an important part of the college application. And the SAT is unlike any exam students will have taken in school. It cannot be mastered by cramming in information or by memorizing enough formulas and vocabulary words. Nevertheless, the skills needed to succeed on this test *can* be developed. The next section offers three very general tips for preparing for the SAT.

3.2 Three Basic Tips for SAT Prep

Over several years of watching and helping tens of thousands of students get through the SAT, I've learned that the three most helpful pieces of advice I can share are almost dismayingly simple...but very powerful.

1. Start early!
2. Practice makes perfect!
3. Practice the right way!

Start early!

The skills necessary to ace the SAT take a long time to develop. Remember, the SAT does not test information retention; it assesses the ability to think and reason critically. And this ability grows over years, not months. Students don't need to know, say, the formula for finding the circumference of a circle. In fact, these basic formulas are provided for students! Rather, students need extensive practice working through different kinds of mathematical problems in order to learn when and how to *use* this formula.

Practice makes perfect!

Some academic skills can only be developed through practice and repetition. The SAT is a timed test. In the Critical Reading section, students might need to read and understand, say, a passage of 850 words from the science section of the *New York Times.* And they'll need to do so in under two minutes. Now it's not possible to improve reading speed overnight. Students need to familiarize themselves with SAT-level reading and vocabulary through extensive and repeated exposure. The best thing that high school freshmen can do to start preparing for the SATs is to develop a daily habit of engaging with advanced material. Just one short article from the *New York Times* daily or one weekly article from the *New Yorker* will work wonders over the next two to three years.

Practice the right way!

Some parents send their students to test prep centers from a very young age, hoping that repeated practice will be enough to raise scores. However, the SAT doesn't just require lots of practice; it demands the right *kind* of practice.

For example, some students diligently complete all their SAT Critical Reading homework with the help of a dictionary. Now learning vocabulary is an important part of preparing for the SATs. However, using a dictionary when doing practice problems is absolutely useless, since students can't take that dictionary with them into the exam! In fact, the SAT doesn't *expect* students to know all the words in a reading passage or a difficult question. Rather, it expects students to use the information they *do* know to *reason* their way to the correct answer. The student who is constantly referring back to the dictionary will never develop this ability.

Here's another example. Many students complete their SAT homework under non-testing conditions. They may spend an hour on a section that would have to be completed in twenty-five minutes in the actual SAT. While slow, careful work is useful for younger students, juniors and seniors must force themselves to work under time pressure.

* * *

Now that students are familiar with the SAT and have some general but tried-and-true strategies for preparing for the test, I'll turn to answer some questions I frequently get asked about the SAT and its precise role in college admissions. As I explained above, the point of the SAT is to provide colleges with a crucial piece of standardized data which can be used to compare students' academic abilities. However, the specific way in which colleges factor in SAT scores differs depending on the caliber (top tier versus lower tiers) and type (public versus private) of school. In the next section, I focus on the way SAT scores are treated at the most selective top-tier colleges.

3.3 The Most Selective Colleges and the SATs

Although, as we saw in chapter one, lots of big-name colleges are breaking rank and no longer requiring that students take the SAT or the ACT, these colleges remain exceptions to what is still very much a rule. Nearly all competitive universities in the U.S., whether public or private, still require applicants to submit standardized test scores as part of the admissions process. This section focuses on the role of the SATs in getting into the *most* selective universities: the Ivy League, Stanford, MIT and Caltech.

What is the value of the SAT at the most selective schools— schools such as, say, Harvard?

The first thing to note is that no college really *likes* the SAT. Schools just accept it as a necessary evil. This is why a very high—even perfect—SAT score alone will never get a student into a top private school. Colleges simply do not put that much value on the information provided by an SAT score.

This means that it is useful to consider the SAT as a basic hurdle. For top private schools, SAT averages tend to be in the low- to mid-700s per section. If a student's SAT scores fall within a school's score range, then that candidate has cleared a minimal hurdle and is now a viable candidate, one who possesses the critical thinking and reasoning skills necessary to succeed at that school. A high SAT score functions as a *basic qualification* rather than a positive asset.

Now I want to be very clear about this. The information above is not designed to diminish the importance of the SAT. Remember: an SAT score *below* a school's score range can rule an applicant out. Unless there are some extraordinary compensatory assets elsewhere in the student profile, the student with the below-average SAT score is simply not going to be a serious candidate.

How many times should a student take the SAT?

Say a student is targeting a top private school, but his or her SAT scores are just not within the average score range of accepted students. Should this student take the SAT again? And how many times?

The magic formula at the most selective schools is, "Take it once but no more than twice." These colleges do not like it when students take and retake the SAT, especially if scores don't significantly improve or—even worse—go up and down. This signifies a lack of ability to use time in an efficient and productive way.

Of course, the SAT is not an easy test. The vast majority of students need consistent test prep to master it. But let's face it. A top school has so many more applicants than it can accept that it can afford to cherry-pick the best of the best. Such schools look for students who are responsible enough to prepare efficiently for the SAT, perceptive enough to take the test only when they are truly ready and—frankly—smart enough to get a great score on just one, at most two, tries.

Students should also avoid retaking the test just to raise their scores a mere forty or fifty points. This is a particular pet peeve of Jon Reider, who was Senior Director of Admissions at Stanford University for over twenty years. Top schools look at students' SAT scores insofar as they fall within a *range* that demonstrates a certain level of critical thinking ability. For example, they do not think there is a significant difference between a 720 on the Writing section and a 740: those twenty points might come down to answering just one more question correctly. Jon Reider considers students who retake the SAT for insignificant score increases "point grubbers" who put too much emphasis on standardized tests at the expense of other, more worthwhile endeavors.[40]

"Super-scoring": How do the most selective schools evaluate scores from multiple sittings?

Many of the most selective schools, including Harvard and Stanford, consider what is called a "super-score": a composite SAT score made up of the student's highest score per subject across multiple sittings.[41] Now the fact that many colleges use the super-score may seem to undercut our advice that students not take the SAT more than two times. Indeed, some students might begin to think that it is to their advantage to take the SAT as many times as possible so as to gain the maximal possible super-score.

However, students must understand that the most selective schools do not *just* look at the SAT super-score. They evaluate a student's entire test-taking *history* to see what it reveals about the student. Some SAT records depict students who have been preoccupied with the SAT and have neglected other interests and activities. Colleges wouldn't find such priorities too attractive. Other SAT records show students who take and retake a test without any decisive improvement. Again, this could reveal inefficiency and unproductiveness.

Should students exercise score choice?

First of all, What is score choice? Score choice is a score-reporting option that allows students to decide which SAT and SAT Subject Test scores to send to colleges. As the College Board puts it, this option was introduced to help students "put

---

[40] Reider, Jon. In personal conversation.

[41] College Board. "SAT® Score-Use Practices by Participating Institution." 24 Sep 2010. Web. 16 Feb 2011.

their best foot forward on test day by giving them more flexibility."[42]

Although most of the big-name schools super-score, not all of them accept score choice. Harvard and Princeton allow students to exercise score choice and select which SAT and SAT Subject Test scores to send. But many of the other most selective schools have rejected score choice. Stanford, for example, requires that students send all of their SAT scores (although students can exercise score choice on the Subject Tests). Columbia and Yale have rejected score choice altogether; they want to see all SAT and SAT Subject Test scores.[43]

Now one question that is hotly debated is, Will colleges know when score choice is being exercised? There is a lot of murkiness around this issue. One thing that is pretty clear is that the College Board cannot send any scores to colleges without the student's permission. If a student elects to send only some of his or her SAT scores to Yale, College Board can't just send *all* of this student's scores to Yale just because Yale has rejected score choice. As the College Board says, "Students are encouraged to follow the score-reporting requirements of each college to which they apply, but their scores will not be released for admission purposes without their specific consent. Colleges and universities will only receive the scores that students send them."[44]

However, this emphatically does *not* mean that students should just exercise score choice with impunity despite a college's express request for full disclosure. First of all, many high schools report SAT scores on a student's transcript. Second of all, the potential consequences of getting caught are extremely severe.

---

[42] College Board. "SAT Score-Reporting Policy." Web. 16 Feb 2011.

[43] College Board. "SAT® Score-Use Practices by Participating Institution." 24 Sep 2010. Web. 16 Feb 2011. Again, students should be sure to verify information directly with colleges.

[44] College Board. "SAT® Score-Use Practices by Participating Institution." Web. 16 Feb 2011. 24 Sep 2010.

It would be fully within the rights of a college or university to cancel an offer of admission, kick out an already-matriculated student, or even revoke an already-granted degree should any dishonesty be revealed. Academic honesty is taken extremely seriously, especially by the most selective institutions, where even unintentional plagiarism is a cause for severe sanction. Students are strongly advised not to try and "game" the admissions office. They should instead focus on developing a test record that they would not *want* to exercise score choice on.

When should I take the SATs?

Top-tier private schools consider more than just SAT scores and the frequency of retakes. They also factor in *when* a student takes the SAT. This little bit of information can provide the admissions officer with an important nugget of insight into the character of the applicant. Here's what I mean.

Admissions officers see so many applications that they accumulate a great wealth of regional information. In particular, they know which areas around the U.S. have an intense test prep culture. So when they open up an application from a student living in, say, northern California, they'll know that this applicant has been inundated with information about the SAT from an early age. So if this student takes the SAT very late—say, at the beginning of senior year—admissions officers will assume that the delay was caused by procrastination rather than a lack of information….and that this applicant has spent the summer before senior year cramming for the SATs, rather than engaging in something more worthwhile.

What this means is that students targeting the most selective private schools should aim to complete their SATs before senior year. Sticking to this timetable will mean that students don't have to waste the crucial summer before senior year on SAT prep, but can pursue more meaningful activities and get a head start on their application essays. It will also mean that students have more information in hand before deciding whether and where to apply early.

*   *   *

This section aimed to give students insight into the role the SATs play in gaining admission to the most selective private schools. I'll summarize with two take-home lessons.

1. Students should remember that attaining a high SAT score is a minimal requirement to get considered for admission, rather than a positive asset that will gain admission. The overwhelming majority of applicants to top private schools come in with excellent SAT scores.

2. Specific SAT scores don't matter as much as a student's score range and test-taking history. A student's SAT score, like his or her GPA, is not just a number. Both are pieces of data that, when analyzed by an admissions officer, yield insights about *character* as much as *aptitude.*

Now I want to emphasize that these two pieces of information are very specific to private school admissions at the most selective institutions nationwide. They don't necessarily apply to other top-tier private schools—prestigious schools like Tufts and NYU—or to public schools. Key differences will be explained in the next section.

3.4 Other Private Schools, Public Schools and the SATs

Let's begin by looking at how the UCs evaluate the SATs. Then we'll turn to see how more selective second-tier schools like Tufts, USC, and Boston College evaluate the SATs.

The UCs and the SATs

In understanding the admissions process for the UCs and most public schools, it's important to keep in mind the sheer numbers of students that we're talking about. A school like UCLA typically receives twice the number of applicants that a comparably-sized private school gets. This means that admissions officers at a UC have that much *less* time to devote to each applicant. As a result, the UC admissions process is much more numbers-driven. In other words, GPA and SAT scores are much more important! Only in very rare cases would an extracurricular activity be able to compensate for low scores. On the flipside, an indifferent extracurricular record probably won't keep a student *out* of a UC, so long as the student maintains high numbers.

The UCs also don't have time to "interpret" SAT test-taking records: they don't have the resources to scrutinize when and how often a particular student has taken a test and work out what this says about the student's character. Rather, the UCs ask for *all* scores and then focus on the highest composite score attained in *one* sitting. Let's say John takes the SAT in October of his junior year and receives a 2100 (700 Math, 700 Critical Reading, 700 Writing). He retakes the SAT in January and receives a 2150 (800 Math, 650 Critical Reading, 700 Writing). The UCs will just focus on the January score in making their admissions decision. In other words, the UCs don't super-score.[45]

Given this information, what is the best SAT test-taking strategy for a student who is targeting the UCs? First of all, this student should take the test as early as possible—probably October of junior year—allowing ample time to retake the test if necessary. Then, this student should retake the test if necessary in order to attain his or her goal score. But students must not abuse this advice and take the SAT before they're really ready—or decide to take the test casually or in a haphazard fashion. There are only a *limited* number of opportunities to take the SATs...and students will need to devote some of these test dates to the SAT Subject Tests. Additionally, SAT test dates routinely coincide with times of high student stress: May and June test dates fall just when students are preparing for AP exams and school finals, and October and November test dates distract students

---

[45] University of California Admissions. "The Examination Requirement." Web. 16 Feb 2011.

preparing their college applications. And of course, all SAT prep must be balanced with schoolwork, since maintaining a strong GPA must be every student's top priority. This means that even students targeting the UCs must be highly strategic and organized about taking the SATs.

Second-tier private colleges and the SATs

Now let's take a look at the SATs in the context of second-tier private schools: schools such as Tufts University, USC and Boston College.

Each of these schools has its own method of evaluating the SAT. Some super-score, some do not; some allow score choice, others do not. Some will spend more time mining the details of an SAT record—how many sittings? how significant the improvements?—for insight into a candidate's character. But whatever the specific method of evaluation, the SAT provides students with a very unique opportunity when it comes to these second-tier universities. Here's what I mean.

As much as they'd like to claim otherwise, the second-tier schools are very sensitive to their rankings in publications such as the *U.S. News & World Report*. While these rankings definitely have their critics, no one would dispute the fact that a high ranking boosts a school's reputation and bumps up applicant numbers. It also pleases college alumni, which in turn can help grow a school's endowment. Now a major factor in coming up with these rankings is the average SAT score of incoming freshmen.

Earlier, we said that students should think of the SAT as a basic hurdle. Scoring within a college's average SAT range is enough to overcome this first hurdle—it's enough to get an applicant on the table as a serious candidate, although not enough to get an applicant in.

However, what about the student with SAT scores that are well above a school's range? This is where the second-tier schools differ significantly from the most selective colleges. At the second-tier schools, a strong SAT score can count as a positive *asset*. Above-average SAT scores will help the college raise its rankings, so colleges have a reason not just to *consider* the student with the high SAT score, but to go ahead and *admit* that student. (In fact, the admissions process at second tier schools is *generally* more forgiving. Demonstrated excellence in one area can more readily compensate for shortcomings in other areas, even GPA.)

By contrast, admissions is so competitive at the most selective schools that there is no room for error. It is pretty much impossible to have an off-the-chart SAT score at a school like Harvard—there are too many 2400s already on the table!

So what's the best SAT test-taking strategy for students targeting a school such as Boston College? Again, students should plan to take the test earlier rather than later to leave enough time to retake the test. Now if a student scores fairly well on their first try—within but not exceeding the target school's average range—then because the student has a reasonable chance of scoring higher on subsequent tries, especially with enough time and due preparation, this student should consider retaking the SAT. However, students and parents must be realistic about the students' ability to improve on the SAT. They must remember that for schools that don't accept score choice, repeated retakes without discernible or significant improvement leave students looking indecisive and unimpressive.

Students should also know that they have an alternative to the SAT. This is the test known as the ACT. I'll discuss this option in the next section.

3.5 The SAT versus the ACT

Previous sections focused on the SAT, the most commonly recognized and widely used standardized college entrance exam. However, there is a second standardized college en-trance exam: the ACT. In this section, I'll explore the differences between the SAT and the ACT and offer some guidelines for deciding which test to take.

From the standpoint of a college admissions officer, the SAT and the ACT are virtually identical. That is, most colleges—including all of the most selective schools and the UCs—do not prefer one test over the other. So students who need to decide which test to take should take the admissions office out of the equation. "Either is fine with us," says Marilyn McGrath-Lewis, Director of Admissions at Harvard University, "and we don't have a feeling that either favors students with any particular profile."[46]

Now most students in California take the SAT. In fact, most of the students who take the ACT live in the Midwest, whereas most of the students opting for the SAT live on either the West Coast or the East Coast. But this geographical distribution has been changing in recent years as the ACT has been steadily gaining in popularity nationwide. An unprecedented 47% of the high school class of 2010 took the ACT, a 30% increase from five years ago.[47] In fact, in 2010, for the first time ever, slightly more college freshmen took the ACT rather than the SAT.[48]

The most important factor in determining whether a student should take the SAT or the ACT is actually quite simple. Students should take the test that best caters to their strengths! The SAT and the ACT each favor different learning styles and test-taking techniques. Therefore, it is very possible that a student who does not do so well on the SAT may excel on the ACT—and vice versa. In order to help students figure out which test better suits them, it's helpful to understand three major differences between the two tests:

1. The two tests differ in overall length, as well as in length of individual sections.

---

[46] Slatalla, Michelle. "Act vs. Sat." *New York Times*. 04 Nov 2007.

[47] "ACT Scores Dip, but More Students Meet College Benchmarks." Associated Press. 18 Aug 2010.

[48] Springen, Karen. "Going SAT-Free." *Newsweek*. 04 Nov 2010.

2. The ACT and SAT assess different abilities: the ACT tests knowledge of a standard high school curriculum; the SAT measures more abstract skills of analytical reasoning developed, but not explicitly taught, in high school.

3. The ACT assumes more mathematical background; it also has a Science section.

Length and structure of test

The SAT is overall a longer test than the ACT: the SAT clocks in at three hours and forty-five minutes, longer than the ACT's two hours and fifty-five minutes (although ACT-takers require an additional thirty minutes if they choose to take the optional writing section—something which, by the way, is highly recommended and in fact *required* by virtually every competitive college that accepts the ACT).

The ACT is divided into fewer but longer sections. The SAT is broken down into ten timed sections (including the un-scored experimental section). By contrast, the ACT only has four sections (five, including the writing section). Depending on the student, one test might feel quite a bit longer than the other. On the one hand, the greater number of sections can make the SAT feel longer. So counselors usually recommend that students with short attention spans or learning disabilities take the ACT. On the other hand, the SAT, which changes pace and subject area more quickly through a greater number of shorter sections, might help some students maintain focus and stay engaged. Each student should consider which test format is better suited to his or her temperament.

Ability being assessed

The SAT has three sections: Critical Reading, Writing and Math. It intends to test a student's *skills*, rather than his or her *knowledge base*. Critical thinking and analytic ability is not something explicitly taught in school, but rather something developed whether a student is studying biology or journalism.

The ACT has four sections: English, Math, Reading and Science. It also has an optional Writing Section. Contrary to the SAT, the ACT is a *curriculum-based* test: it tests a student's mastery of *content*. In the words of the ACT test-designer, "the questions on the ACT are directly related to what students have learned in high school courses in English, mathematics, and science."[49]

The SAT suits one type of student and the ACT another. The general consensus among high school counselors is that "bright underachievers" tend to do better on the SAT. In other words, students who tend to rely on "smarts" and intuition rather than a teacher's explanation usually have the strong critical reasoning skills necessary to work through the subtleties of the SAT.

"Hard workers," on the other hand, tend to do better on the ACT. These are students who make above-average grades not because they are necessarily the quickest students in a class, but because they put in the most effort. Such students tend to do better on the ACT because it is more similar to tests given at school. These students will tend to find questions on the ACT more straightforward, whereas SAT questions can seem less clear-cut, even "tricky."

Differences in content

The SAT Math section covers up to Geometry and Algebra 2. The ACT Math section covers up to Trigonometry.

Additionally, the ACT includes a Science section. This is not an information-based exam in the same way that the SAT Subject Tests or AP Exams in the sciences are. Rather, the ACT checks a student's ability to analyze charts, for example, or otherwise engage in scientific reasoning. In other words, students do not

---

[49] ACT. "Facts About the ACT." Web. 17 Feb 2011.

need any special or specific scientific background to successfully answer the questions on the Science portion of the ACT.

*   *   *

The information given above can help students evaluate whether they are better suited for the ACT or the SAT, but the most accurate way for students to figure this out is for them to take a diagnostic SAT *and* a diagnostic ACT under simulated test conditions. Many tutoring centers, including FLEX, offer free diagnostic testing. It is important for students to figure out which test is right for them early on—ideally, I recommend that students take diagnostic tests early on in their sophomore years—so they can tailor their test prep accordingly.

In some cases, however, it might be worth a student's while to take *both* the SAT and the ACT. For example, one student I knew, Diane, took SAT classes for six months and raised her score almost 400 points, eventually scoring 1960 on the actual exam. Although she dramatically improved her score, she felt she hadn't realized her potential and thought she'd be able to substantially raise that score in subsequent exams. However, we counseled her to take a stab at the ACT instead. The ACT really catered to Diane's strengths, and she received a 33: the equivalent of a 2200 on the SAT!

Now compare Diane's friend, Tara. Tara also took the SAT when Diane did, but Tara received a 2040 on her first attempt. Satisfied with this score, she never retook the test or tried the ACT. Apart from their standardized test scores, the girls were virtually identical. Their GPAs were nearly equivalent and their course selection very similar. Their activities were also comparable; if anything, Tara's activities were slightly stronger than Diane's. However, when the college admissions letters came back, Diane got into a bunch of schools that Tara was rejected from, including Boston College and NYU. Why? Tara had the higher SAT score but Diane had the higher standardized test score.

Deciding whether to take the SAT or the ACT is a very personal choice. Students shouldn't be affected by local trends; they should rely on accurate diagnostic testing and find the test that best showcases their strengths.

3.6 SAT Subject Tests

As a college counselor, I see a lot of confusion surrounding the SAT Subject Tests (formerly—and still commonly—known as the SAT IIs). For many students, these tests, as well as the AP exams, just don't register as that important, and so some students don't spend a lot of time preparing for them.

This attitude is, to a certain extent, perfectly understandable. Although almost all colleges still require the SAT or the ACT, requirements for SAT Subject Tests are highly variable. Lots of schools no longer require the SAT Subject Tests at all. The California State University system hasn't demanded SAT Subject Test scores for a long time. The UC system just recently followed suit and got rid of their SAT Subject Test requirement: students applying to UCs from the high school class of 2012 onwards no longer have to submit any SAT Subject Test scores. Nor is this just a public school phenomenon. USC doesn't require the submission of SAT Subject Test scores. And for a highly prestigious example, we can add Stanford to our list.

A word of caution is in order here. Just because schools such as USC and Stanford don't *require* the SAT Subject Tests, it doesn't follow that students should not take them. On the contrary, in my experience, the vast majority of successful USC applicants *did* take *at least* two Subject Tests. And both the UCs and Stanford University explicitly *recommend* that applicants submit the results of at least two SAT Subject Test scores.

Other colleges have still different policies surrounding the SAT Subject Tests. Claremont McKenna College, a highly selective liberal arts college in southern California, only requires homeschooled students to submit SAT Subject Test scores (one in math, one in any other subject).[50] But Pomona College, right down the street from Claremont McKenna, requires that students who are submitting the SAT *also* submit scores from two SAT Subject Tests in different fields. (Students also have the option of submitting just an ACT score in lieu of the three SAT scores.)[51]

Not only do different universities have very different SAT Subject Test requirements, certain majors or special degree programs often have specific Subject Test requirements. For example, students applying to study engineering are often required to submit scores from one of the two math and one of the three science SAT Subject Tests. And even when this is not explicitly required, admissions officers will certainly expect aspiring engineers to have taken at least some of these tests and will look closely at any test scores in these subjects.

As this brief sampling of admissions requirements reveals, there is a wide variety of policies with regard to the SAT Subject Tests—and these policies are constantly being reevaluated and altered. This means that it is extremely important for students and their parents to carefully research the requirements at their target universities. It also means that deciding which tests to take is not a simple matter.

Having said that, I can still offer some general suggestions. First of all, when a particular SAT Subject Test is *required,* it takes on a higher priority. For example, students applying to MIT are required to take one of the math SAT Subject Tests. Now among successful applicants to MIT, 75% had math scores of 750+. What does this mean? Remember that having an SAT test that falls within a college's range of admitted SAT scores is a minimal hurdle candidates have to pass to be seriously considered. For candidates at MIT, attaining a 750+ in the Math 2 Subject Test should be considered a comparable *minimal* hurdle. Students

---

[50] Claremont McKenna College Admissions. "Applying to CMC." Web. 17 Feb 2011.

[51] Pomona College Admissions. "Testing Requirement." Web. 17 Feb 2011.

who do not meet that criterion must have something exceptional elsewhere on their application to make up for their below-average SAT Subject Test score.

Also, students can use the Subject Tests to demonstrate their interests or highlight their strengths. Candidates who have special aptitude in learning foreign languages, for example, might choose to demonstrate this through SAT Subject Tests, especially if they haven't taken these languages in school and so can't prove their level of mastery through grades.

Students can also use the Subject Tests to compensate *in part* for a weak school grade. Say Ben is a student who has been pulling As, with the occasional B+, in his science classes. However, he really struggles the first semester of his Physics class and ends up with a B–. Now Ben might want to focus his energies on really acing the SAT Physics test. A very strong score—say, a 770—will prove to admissions officers that he has mastered the material. It will also show character: instead of trying to avoid a subject he has found challenging, Ben has obviously decided to dig in and really fight to master the stuff. However, students shouldn't rely on this option too much or over-exercise it. Even a perfect SAT Subject Test score can't fully make up for poor schoolwork. And students with high SATs but lots of low grades showcase their intelligence at the expense of their character: they're evidently smart students who are nevertheless irresponsible and disengaged in their day-to-day schoolwork.

What about students who don't fall under any of the categories above: students who don't have specific majors or colleges in mind, or who don't know where their academic interests lie, or who don't have other pressing reasons to focus their energies on any particular SAT Subject Test? At the broadest level of generality, I advise students who hope to be competitive at top-tier private colleges to aim to secure at least two, ideally three strong SAT Subject Test scores in different areas (one in math or science, and one in the humanities). However, I stress that the details of each student's academic history and goals will influence what it is right for that student to do when it comes to the SAT subject tests. In the next and last section of this chapter, I'll present a case study to bring together and illustrate the topics discussed so far.

3.7 Case Study:
Jane's SAT Subject Test Dilemma

Jane was a Chinese-American student who attended a highly competitive public high school near Los Angeles and, although a second generation U.S. citizen, was reasonably proficient in the Chinese language. Sound familiar?

Now Jane wanted to know which SAT Subject Tests she should take. More specifically, she wanted to know whether she should take the SAT Subject Test in Chinese.

Because Jane had grown up in a Chinese-speaking household, she was reasonably confident that she would be able to score very highly on the Chinese test. In fact, she was pretty sure she could secure a perfect 800. However, she was wary of how top-tier colleges would view her choice of exam. Since admissions officers would be familiar with her background and ethnicity, she thought she might be penalized for taking an "easy" exam. Taking all these factors into consideration, should Jane have taken the Chinese subject test?

First of all, is the Chinese Subject Test really considered an "easy" test? Yes. Not all SAT scores are created equal. Every SAT score is accompanied by a second number: the percentile rank. Now the percentile rank for an 800 on the Chinese SAT is 57%, while the percentile rank for an 800 on the Spanish SAT is 95%.[52] What does this mean? This means that the student who aced the Spanish test did better than 95% of all students who took the test—a real achievement. However, the student who

---

[52] College Board. "SAT Subject Tests^{TM} Percentile Ranks, 2010 College-Bound Seniors." Web. 17 Feb 2011.

aced the Chinese SAT only did better than 57% of all students who took the test. That is, more than two out of every five students who took the Chinese SAT *also* got an 800! Obviously, the Spanish test score is a much more significant achievement. What accounts for this huge difference in percentile rank? The simple fact—well known to college admissions officers—that the overwhelming majority of students who take the Chinese SAT are ethnic Chinese, and most of them will have been raised in households where at least some Chinese was spoken.

With that information in hand, we can better evaluate Jane's situation. But we still need to distinguish again between private and public school admissions. We should also factor in Jane's choice of major.

Let's consider the UCs first. Remember that the UCs no longer require SAT Subject Tests. Therefore, an 800 on the Chinese test would be something over and beyond what is necessary to apply to the UCs. It would generally *help* Jane in the UC application process. However, Jane really wanted to get into UCLA, one of the most competitive UCs, and she wanted to get into one of the most competitive schools at UCLA: the School of Engineering and Applied Science. Now although the UCs don't require the SAT Subject Tests, they still recommend it. And to be sure, students looking to get into one of the most competitive UCs should be following these recommendations! For Jane to really give the UCLA School of Engineering her best shot, she needed to secure two strong SAT Subject Tests *not* including the Chinese test. An 800 on Chinese would be great as a third test— but for her primary two tests, we recommended that she stick with Math 2 and one of the science tests.

Now let's turn to Jane's private school aspirations. As we explained earlier, each private school has its own specific requirements for standardized test scores. However, we can make some broad generalizations with regards to Jane's situation. Although an 800 on the Chinese SAT was not going to be considered as much of an achievement as an 800 on almost any other Subject Test, the score wouldn't be entirely meaningless. Getting a great score on a standardized test score never hurts! In fact, if Jane wanted to study International Relations or East Asian Studies, her demonstrated proficiency in the Chinese language could have added strength to her application. However, in order to remain competitive at the most selective private universities, Jane needed to take at least two *further* SAT Subject Tests in core academic areas. That way her 800 in Chinese wouldn't be competing against another student's 800 in, say, Chemistry.

As for which two core Subject Tests Jane should take, she needed to do some research to figure this out. The Engineering Department at Princeton, for example, requires students take either Math 1 or Math 2 and either Physics or Chemistry.[53] The UCs, on the other hand, did not accept Math 1 even when they required two SAT Subject Tests.

After I spelled all of this information out for Jane, I had her take a diagnostic test in Chinese. Jane scored a 720—a good starting score, but several weeks' work away from an 800. So Jane decided not to waste her time preparing for the Chinese test, but focused instead on the Math 2 and the Chemistry tests. Scores of 750+ on both of these tests were strong enough to get her into UCLA and Cornell.

*　　*　　*

In this chapter, I tried to dispel some of the misconceptions surrounding standardized tests. Of course the SATs and the ACT are important tests: strong performances are necessary for students to be realistic candidates at the most selective schools, and they can really help students looking to secure entrance to a top-notch public school or any other private school. However, students mustn't overestimate the importance of the SAT. And they shouldn't pin unrealistic hopes on an excellent score, or exhaust themselves retaking the test over and over for negligible

---

[53] Princeton University School of engineering and Applied Science Undergraduate Admissions. "Prospective Students FAQ." Web. 17 Feb 2011.

score increases. Students should simply start preparing early—and they should always prepare smartly. Doing this will ensure that they test at potential when it matters.

Chapter 4:
Extracurricular Activities

How important are extracurricular activities in the college application process? Simply: extracurricular activities are *at least* as important as students have been told—especially when it comes to private school admissions. In chapter one, I gave a rough illustration of how admissions works at a school like Stanford University. Of 32,000 applications, around 23,000 will possess the academic qualification necessary to succeed. But only 2,400 students will end up getting accepted! This means that Stanford will deny admission to around 20,600 academically qualified students: students with near-perfect GPAs and stellar standardized test scores. So what distinguishes the select 2,400 from the remaining 20,600? Extracurricular activities!

Unfortunately, this part of the college admissions process is not only highly important, it is also surrounded by a good deal of misinformation. This chapter will go behind the myths and explain what really catches a college's attention and what colleges are really looking for when they examine a student's extracurricular record. Before I get started, though, I'm going to set an introductory exercise for parents.

4.1 An Introductory Exercise for Parents

Parents should take a moment to answer the following questions *honestly*:

- Are you seeing the same parents when you go to your kid's speech and debate tournaments as when you pick up your kid from orchestra rehearsal?

- Did you sign your son up for that particular Boy Scout troop because Mrs. Kim's son got his Eagle Scout badge there…right before heading off to the University of Pennsylvania?

- Are you worried that your daughter should stop concentrating so much on studio art because all the other kids you know are working on the school newspaper?

- Are your kids more excited to go on that mission trip to Mexico because they think they can make a real difference…or because all of their friends are going, too?

Now stop and visualize all those familiar faces following your kid to band camp, church, even SAT class. These kids are the competition. What do you think will happen if your kid looks just like the competition?

One of the top questions I hear from parents is, Which extracurricular activity will get my kid into such-and-such college? This is in many ways exactly the wrong question to ask. There is no such thing as *the* ideal extracurricular activity, because there is no such thing as *the* ideal college applicant. College admissions officers admit *individuals*, not ideals, and they treat extracurricular activities as reflections of an individual's unique interests and passions. They look to admit students who will be able to come together to form a cohesive community but *diverse* community.

However, although there's no such thing as *the* ideal extracurricular activity, there *is* such a thing as the *wrong* activity. The wrong activity, as the above exercise shows, is the activity chosen *because everyone else is doing it* or *because it got so-and-so into Cornell.*

This doesn't mean that a student should *not* participate in, say, speech and debate just because it's a trendy activity, or that a student should pick the bassoon over the violin just because it's a less popular instrument. The key to building a successful extracurricular record is to identify a student's *genuine* interests. If a student's passion is in fact speech and debate, then, by all means, the student should excel at speech and debate! However, parents should avoid molding their kids' activities to fit some preconceived ideal they believe colleges are looking for. This does a real disservice to the student. In all my years of counseling, I haven't encountered a single student who isn't a true individual. However, all that uniqueness gets lost as soon as I look at that student on paper. Unfortunately, for many admissions officers, their only chance to "meet" the student is on the written page. They have to go by what they're given—and what they're given are too many carbon copies of the same high-achieving but ultimately undistinguishable student.

This chapter is dedicated to giving students and their parents—especially those who caught a glimpse of themselves in the exercise above—the information they need to develop their extracurricular profiles. In the next section, I'll explain what admissions officers are looking for. What do extracurricular activities tell them? And what do colleges really like to see? Then I'll offer concrete tips for developing an extracurricular profile at various stages of the college preparation process, from freshman year—or even middle school—through senior year. My advice will be illustrated with a bunch of case studies.

Before we get started, a word of encouragement. I urge students and their parents not to look upon this part of the college admission process with undue trepidation. This is where things get fun! It's not too much of an over-simplification to say that students just need to discover where their passions lie...and then do what they love.

4.2 What Admissions Officers Look For

Remember that when admissions officers evaluate student applications, they are looking for answers to the questions, Who is this student? and What makes him or her different from everyone else? Getting detailed answers to these questions is greatly important to colleges for lots of reasons. First of all, colleges need to select students who are minimally capable of succeeding at the college. Second of all, colleges want to find students who will mesh with the campus culture and philosophy—students who can come together in a cohesive community. But lastly, colleges don't want a class of clones. They want a community that embraces diversity, a community made up of unique individuals who have things to learn from each other.

Now the academic parts of the application—GPA and SAT or ACT scores—go a long way to answering the two questions above. They tell colleges a good deal about a student's academic aptitude and intellectual interests; they also, as we've seen, provide more than a few hints about a student's academic character. So what does a student's extracurricular activities add to this picture?

Extracurricular records give admissions officers a sense of students' idiosyncratic and unique interests. Although there are only so many variations to the high school curriculum, and although students can only choose from so many testing options, extracurricular records can be utterly original.

The truly impressive extracurricular record, however, stands out not because there's something there that nobody else has ever done. After all, as the saying goes, there's nothing truly new under the sun! The truly impressive extracurricular record stands out because it's a record of a student's *passions*, rather than a list of hobbies. Genuine passion can't be faked. It can be attested to by the amount of time and energy that a student dedicates to pursuing an activity, or the imagination and creativity with which the student engages in a project, or by the student's incessant commitment to finding ways to share certain experiences with others.

Our case studies below will help students understand how passion comes through in an extracurricular résumé. But first, here are four additional things that admissions officers like to see in a student's extracurricular record:

1. Breadth and depth
2. Volunteerism
3. Leadership and initiative
4. Local participation and action
5. A global perspective

Breadth and depth

Broadly speaking, there are two types of extracurricular profiles I see: the student who only does a few things but does them "deeply" and the student who does a lot of things but does all of them "superficially." The first student has depth; the second breadth.

What do colleges prefer? "I look at a student's ability to be committed to an activity, as well as depth and level of accomplishment," says Jim Montoya, Stanford University's former Dean of Admissions.[54] Stanford's admissions office elaborates on this on its website. "Students often assume that our primary concern is the number of activities in which you participate. In fact, an exceptional depth of experience in one or two activities may demonstrate your passion more than minimal participation in five or six clubs. We want to see the impact you have had on that club, in your school, or in the larger community,

---

[54] Stanford University News Service. "Dean Explains What Wins College Admission." 01 Feb 1992. Web. 17 Feb 2011.

and we also want to learn of the impact that experience has had on you."[55]

What this means is that, with the exception of students with truly outstanding talents (the nationally-ranked golfer, for example), colleges typically want to see students falling somewhere in between the two types we introduced above. Students should have some defining passion, but they should also be three-dimensional, well-rounded individuals. There is no need for students to load up on activities that they don't care about: students shouldn't feel that they need to participate in a sport *and* play an instrument *and* paint on the side *and* have a pet "cause." The important thing is for students to have something they really enjoy and something they really care about.

It is also important for students to display two specific character traits in their extracurricular activities: persistence and integrity. People often say, "Finish what you start." That's true of extracurricular activities. While students don't have to pursue everything for four straight years, they do want to demonstrate that they see things through, whether it's a menial summer job or a commitment to tutoring for a year.

Community service and volunteerism

Colleges like to see students engage with their communities and try to make a difference. This means that students should strive to take each of their major activities and add some community-service dimension to it. This will have the added benefit of drawing close connections between a student's different activities and adding cohesion to a student's extracurricular record as a whole.

For example, many students who play musical instruments participate in fundraising concerts. Others might teach music to underprivileged children in the community. These are great ways

---

[55] Stanford University Undergraduate Admission. "Application Evaluation." Web. 17 Feb 2011.

of using talents to give back to the community. They also serve to link together a student's community service and artistic activities, portraying a student who brings everything learned in one area of life to bear on all the other parts of life.

Leadership and initiative

In the past few years, we have seen the word "initiative" replace the word "leadership" as the big buzz word in admissions. But that's because leadership is often misunderstood. It's often confused with titles; therefore, many students seek positions with titles that don't seem to mean very much and don't lead to noticeable results.

Real leadership, on the other hand, involves initiative. It's displayed when students actually take action and drive change. At its best, it is creative, courageous and risk-taking. There are obvious reasons why colleges are impressed by students who display genuine leadership. Students who possess this elusive trait in high school will be sure to be leaders on and off campus.

Here's an example of poor leadership. Bill is president of the Spanish club. The Spanish club meets once a week in the Spanish teacher's room for lunch. This activity is relatively valueless on the college application. Now if Bill were to develop this into a lunch-time exchange program, for example, with another school that has a lot of native Spanish-speaking ESL students, then this activity would suddenly have "impact" and Bill would be acting as a real leader.

Taking action and participating locally...

Jeffrey Brenzel, former Dean of Admissions at Yale, says that when colleges evaluate extracurricular activities, they "try to understand the student as a whole person, and also to understand how he or she has performed *in the context of whatever academic and community opportunities he or she has encountered.*"[56] The qualifier "in the context" is very important. Let me explain.

Students are always encouraged to take advantage of the opportunities available to them in their own schools and communities. Whether seeking leadership opportunities or honors and awards, the first place a student should start is his or her own school. Why? Because colleges want students who will actively and eagerly contribute to the life of the college community.

For example, lots of students participate in speech and debate. But I get some students who, rather than joining their school speech and debate teams, go to expensive tutoring centers and private enrichment programs. Now the only person who benefits from this is the student, who could just as easily develop his or her skills on the school team, helping out teammates and bringing credit to the school at the same time. On the same note, I see lots of students who say that writing is their passion but don't contribute to the school literary magazine or newspaper. Where's the evidence of the passion?

Participating in opportunities made available at school and locally can also lend credibility to a student's achievements and attest to the student's talents. For example, accruing honors in privately-organized speech and debate programs can't compare to winning awards at school speech and debate tournaments, which are held up to *nationally*-established standards.

...but seeking a global perspective

The world really is getting smaller and smaller every day. It is important for students to remain informed world citizens with a basic understanding of what's going on around the world and how most of the world lives. They may be surprised to know how much this matters. I've read lots of well-meaning admissions

---

[56] Shor, Melanie. "College Admissions Myths." *Forbes.* 14 Sep 2006. Italics added.

essays in which the student's lack of perspective is painfully obvious...and ultimately harmful.

Seth Allen, the Dean of Admission and Financial Aid at Grinnell College—a highly-selective Midwestern college—can't forget one applicant who wrote about her experience volunteering in China in the wake of the 2008 earthquake. "Every day, I showered and brushed my teeth using cold water," this applicant wrote. "It was unbearable."[57] We can guess how this candidate fared!

Whether by taking courses or by traveling or by participating in a service activity with a global reach (fundraising for worldwide disaster relief, for example), students should seek to broaden their horizons. They should balance activism within their local communities with an honest attempt to educate themselves about the greater world around them.

4.3 The Importance of Planning Ahead

Students nowadays don't have it easy. They must maintain near-perfect GPAs while juggling AP-heavy school schedules; they have to maximize their test scores while developing an extracurricular profile that distinguishes them from all the other students with near-perfect GPAs and impeccable test scores. As William Damon, Professor of Education at Stanford, says, "Everyone on every admissions committee I know says, 'Thank God I'm not applying to school these days.' How do these kids do so much?"[58]

Although Professor Damon's question was rhetorical, we can actually answer it. Those students who do manage to achieve "so much" have planned well...and they've planned well ahead. We've all heard the saying. "Rome wasn't built in a day." In the

---

[57] Steinberg, Jacques. "Recruiting in China Pays Off for U.S. Colleges." *New York Times.* 11 Feb 2011.

[58] Williams, Alex. "Lost Summer for the College-Bound." *New York Times.* 04 Jun 2006.

same way, students must lay the foundation for extracurricular activities from the moment they start high school—if not sooner.

To get an overview of how students should approach this multi-year project, it'll help to understand how extracurricular activities are reported to colleges. Here's the Activities section of the Common Application (or Common App, for short). This is the primary private college application used nationwide, available at www.commonapp.org:

ACTIVITIES

Extracurricular Please list your principal extracurricular, community, volunteer and family activities and hobbies in the order of their interest to you. Include specific events and/or major accomplishments such as musical instrument played, varsity letters earned, etc. To allow us to focus on the highlights of your activities, please complete this section even if you plan to attach a résumé.

Grade level or post-graduate (PG)					Approximate time spent		When did you participate in the activity?		Positions held, honors won, or letters earned	If applicable, do you plan to participate in college?
9	10	11	12	PG	Hours per week	Weeks per year	School year	Summer		
○	○	○	○	○	____	____	○	○		○
Activity										
○	○	○	○	○	____	____	○	○	_____	○
Activity										
○	○	○	○	○	____	____	○	○		○
Activity										

Students are instructed to indicate how many hours per week and how many weeks per year they engage in an activity and to specify whether the activity is a school-year or summer activity. And students are invited to *order* this list, from most to least important. Obviously, a student with lots of random activities and no overriding passions or clear interests will find this hard to do!

(Note that the Common App has a separate section called Honors, falling under the Academics part of the application, which asks students to list academic prizes and awards. Now many students pursue extracurricular activities related to their academic interests. This is a great way to explore potential careers and majors; it also demonstrates a love of learning. However, these academically-related activities should be listed in the Honors section rather than the Activities section. For example, membership in the National Honor Society or the California Scholarship Federation should be noted under Honors.

84

The same goes for participation in academic competitions, such as the AMC or AIME. The Activities section of the Common App should be treated as a place for students to showcase *non-academic* interests. This is where colleges get answers to critical questions such as, Where will this student fit in our school community? and What will this student contribute to the school community?)

For students reading this early enough—students who still have some time to develop their extracurricular profiles—adopting a focused application strategy *now* is crucial. Starting early enough will ensure that students end up with a coherent, well-ordered list of projects and passions by the time applications are due. The timetable below summarizes what students should aim for at various stages of the process:

- 9th-10th grade: Sign up for lots of activities to explore as many options as possible.

- 10th-11th grade: Start narrowing down and focusing activities. Keep a lookout for leadership opportunities.

- 11th-12th grade: Draw connections between activities and undertake leadership roles. Plan and execute a defining project the summer before senior year.

Freshmen should explore lots of different activities. They should gain exposure to as many things as possible: sports, music, art, various kinds of community service, academic enrichment activities, etc. The goal is to discover talents and interests. If students leave 9th grade with just one or two activities that have really captured their imagination, they'll have had a successful freshman year.

In the summer after freshman year, students still have time to try new pursuits. But they should start thinking about trimming down their commitments and focusing their energies. I also recommend that students find some summer activity that can carry over into the school year and be pursued within the school environment.

Sophomores should start focusing more intensely on select projects and activities. And as they approach the end of 10th grade, sophomores must start becoming *strategic*. Most leadership opportunities become available to juniors, so students who want to earn such positions must be in position by the end of sophomore year.

The summer before junior year should also be put to good use. Some of the most impressive summer activities span two summers. A first summer is used to establish a project, get informed and explore options; the second responds to the limitations and failures of the first year's project. For example, lots of students go on a mission trip the summer before junior year. Often this trip is organized by their church and students just kind of go along with things. However, some students—those with initiative—come back with fresh ideas. Maybe one student will be motivated to raise money throughout the school year to refurbish the playground at the school he or she volunteered at. Perhaps another might start a letter-exchange program between kids in Mexico and kids at church. These projects can be "grown" over the school year and organically give rise to a much more significant and highly personal summer activity the next year.

Rising juniors and seniors should already have identified defining passions. They need to position themselves to develop these interests in meaningful ways and to exercise leadership. This takes foresight and groundwork. Juniors should be thinking about some capstone project that can serve as the defining moment in their extracurricular record. Ideally, as we saw above, this project will naturally emerge of previous summer activities and projects. Upperclassmen should also find ways to demonstrate perseverance, character and initiative in their activities.

The summer before senior year is the most critical summer for students' college admissions. It really *defines* a student's extracurricular profile. This means that students must choose how to spend their time wisely and they must be aggressive in pursuing opportunities made available to them. All their efforts should climax in a project that stretches their leadership and organizational skills and pushes them out of their safety zones.

In the sections to come, I offer some further concrete advice on how to develop extracurricular records. A lot depends on what year the student is in. Obviously, the earlier the student is in his or her high school career, the more options remain open. The next section focuses on selecting suitable summer projects. Then I'll address freshmen, sophomores, juniors and seniors separately, using case studies to illustrate my advice.

4.4 Summer Activities

During the school year, homework and exams, not to mention SAT prep, sports, and school orchestra rehearsals, take over a high school student's calendar. So when can a student find time to invest in really meaningful extracurricular activities? Summers are obviously the only extensive blocks of free time students have. This means that summers must be wisely spent and carefully planned for. In this section I'll answer three frequently asked questions about summer activities.

1. Should a student's activities be closely related to his or her intended major?

2. How much time should a student invest in summer activities?

3. Is it worthwhile to start a new activity the summer before senior year?

Should students' activities be related to their intended college major?

The most important thing is for a student's summer activity to be integrated with the rest of his or her profile *as a whole*, not that it relate specifically to the student's *academic* interests.

Many students don't have a very clear idea of what they're going to major in. For such students, summer activities should express their current priorities and interests. Take Sam, a student vaguely interested in majoring in political science, international business, maybe even pre-law. Though he doesn't have a clear view of his future, he does have a very strong set of current interests. He's always been into learning about other cultures and has traveled quite a bit and picked up two foreign languages. Now Sam can choose between taking a summer law course at the University of Chicago or going back to Peru to engage in a community-service project and further develop his Spanish skills. What should he do? Sam's summer activity should integrate with his well-developed extracurricular priorities, rather than *possible* future college major. Sam should go to Peru.

But there are other students who have a very clear idea of what they want to do in college. These students will, in all likelihood, have already focused their extracurricular activities on *academic* activities. For example, Amy knew from very early on that she wanted to become a doctor. She aggressively piled up biomedical research internships every summer and hospital volunteer work every school year. Amy's summer activity will link up with her future college major—but it will also integrate with her extracurricular activities.

How much time should a student invest in summer activities?

Time is a student's most precious commodity. Regardless of whether high school students will agree to this, they absolutely apply it in their own lives: students inevitably find time to spend on the things that they enjoy the most. I've known countless students who are "too tired" to practice the piano or read a novel after completing their homework. But no matter what time those students close their books, they inevitably have enough energy and interest to go online, update their Facebook page, play video games or watch Manga videos. Why? Because students love those activities. Some parents have told me that their children can sit in front of a computer for ten to twelve hours at a time without getting up to get a drink or use the bathroom. Now, *that's* passion!

It's unsurprising, then, that colleges often consider the number of hours a student devotes to a project a rough measure of his or her passion. Obviously, students can only spend so many hours a week pursuing extracurricular activities during the school year. But how much time should they devote to these activities during the summer? The right answer to this question varies from student to student. But as a general rule of thumb, I counsel my students as follows:

1. Set aside around eight hours per day for college-prep related activities, whether studying or pursuing extracurricular activities. Remember: eight hours a day is not all that much time! It is roughly equivalent to the number of hours students spend in school during the school year. Even students who need to sleep ten hours a day will be left with six hours of free time daily!

2. Eight-hour days spread over a ten-week vacation yields 400-500 hours of total work over a summer. Wisely spent, this can generate really astonishing results.

3. Identify all the major tasks to be accomplished during the summer and then prioritize them, making sure to allocate enough time to the higher priority activities. It's far better to cut down on commitments and follow through completely on the remaining ones than to end up with poorly-done or half-complete jobs all around.

4. Set specific goals and deadlines for all activities. Don't work aimlessly, killing time. Rather, create a plan so that every task achieves something. It's better not to work at all than to work pointlessly!

Is it worthwhile to start a new activity the summer before senior year?

To answer this question, we must first define "new." Students who have been involved with a particular activity throughout high school naturally end up with a coherent, personal story to tell. At the very least, admissions officers will see a consistent commitment to this activity. At best, they'll see an interest steadily cultivated and eventually flourishing into a passion. For students with such long-standing and well-developed interests, the summer before senior year is the time to take things to the next level. They may start something "new" so long as it connects organically with their other activities and maintains continuity.

These students would be able to present their extracurricular histories in the following way on the Common Application:

EXTRACURRICULAR ACTIVITIES & WORK EXPERIENCE

Extracurricular Please list your principal extracurricular, volunteer, and work activities in their order of importance to you. Feel free to group your activities and paid work experience separately if you prefer. Use the space available to provide details of your activities and accomplishments (specific events, varsity letter, musical instrument, employer, etc.) To allow us to focus on the highlights of your activities, please complete this section even if you plan to attach a résumé.

Grade level or post-graduate (PG)					Approximate time spent		When did you participate in the activity?			Positions held, honors won, letters earned, or employer	If applicable, do you plan to participate in college?
9	10	11	12	PG	Hours per week	Weeks per year	School year	Summer/ School Break			
○	○	○	○	○	10	20	○	○	Conclusion		○
Activity											
○	○	○	○	○	25	8	○	○	Climax of story		○
Activity											
○	○	○	○	○	4	40	○	○	Introduction: how student got involved in the activity		○
Activity											

Of course, some students will not have been involved with any activities at all during high school. Such students will obviously *have* to start brand new activities the summer before senior year, investing as much time and energy as possible into making those activities meaningful despite the brevity of their engagement with these activities. Better late than never.

Hopefully, though, most of my readers aren't in such straits. The next few sections are directed at students at earlier stages of the admissions process. They're intended to make sure students don't end up having to fabricate new interests right before college applications are in. I'll start by addressing freshmen and then work my way up to seniors, using case studies to make my points.

4.5 Advice for Freshmen (and Middle School Students)

This is my favorite age group to counsel. Freshmen (and younger students) still have their whole future in front of them. With a little foresight and the right advice, they can create an ideal high school experience for themselves, not only in academic terms but also when it comes to extracurricular activities.

For example, freshmen still have time to make informed, unhurried decisions about when they will take their standardized tests and when they should start preparing for them. Postponing thinking about these things until sophomore or, even worse, junior year piles on stress, just when everything else is becoming harder. Think about it. Junior-year students have to take the most difficult classes…and yet junior-year grades matter more than any other grades so far! Add to that the need to prepare for and ace a bunch of standardized tests and the pressures of trying to come up with significant extracurricular activities. My point is that there is a lot just ahead of the curve. Savvy freshmen will inform themselves about what's coming and plan ahead! The more they accomplish as freshmen, the more they'll save up of that most valuable of commodities that upperclassmen never have enough of: time.

In particular, there are three things that I always advise eighth and ninth graders to try and accomplish. These suggestions might seem irrelevant to the college process. However, having pored over thousands of applications, I can promise that students who do the following will have a significant advantage over their peers. Students just starting their high school careers should:

1. Establish good habits.
2. Search actively for their true passions.
3. Make the right friends.

Let's discuss these in more detail.

Establish good habits.

Now is the time for students to cut the tether to the Internet, phone and TV. Students need to develop discipline *before* they really need it.

Students should also actively seek to develop effective study habits. And they should address any academic weaknesses *before* coursework starts becomes more advanced. Students with a weak grasp of grammar will want to develop their writing skills *before* they have to produce ten-page AP U.S. History research papers. Students with a shaky grasp of Algebra I will want to solidify their mathematical foundation *before* entering Algebra II. Once students are floundering in a difficult class, it's too late: they'll forever be playing catch-up.

Discover passions.

Not everything a student does his or her freshman year is merely a preparation for future years, however. Freshman year is also meant to be a year of exploration and self-discovery, a time when students can try various things and discover their true passions.

To that end, I highly encourage students to take full advantage of the activities and clubs offered at their schools. These clubs are readily accessible and allow students to "try out" various activities.

I also tell motivated students to use the summer before freshman and/or sophomore grade to enroll in programs such as the Johns

Hopkins Center for Talented Youth (CTY) or Stanford's Education Program for Gifted Youth (EPGY). These enrichment programs allow bright students to study non-standard academic subjects in a challenging and creative environment. Students can see whether their curiosity about, say, oceanography—a subject that can't really be studied in high school—is a passing fancy or a genuine passion.

Of course, in trying to discover new interests, students shouldn't neglect those talents they've worked so many years to develop. Top-notch musicians, athletes, even Eagle Scouts aren't created in the space of a high school career. Freshmen should continue building on those activities that they've been participating in all along, especially if they are passionate about or gifted in a particular area.

Make the right friends.

Last but not least: students should know that who their friends are can make a huge difference in what opportunities are open to them four years down the line. We're all social beings, highly influenced by those around us. As freshmen prepare to navigate some of the most rigorous and demanding years of their lives, they need likeminded friends: peers with whom to exchange information about opportunities and resources, classmates who can keep them motivated and push them onwards through some friendly competition.

4.6 Advice for Sophomores

Although sophomores have a lot more to juggle than freshmen, they still have some time and freedom to figure out where their passions lie. But by the end of sophomore year—and in time for the summer after sophomore year—students should be ready to commit to certain activities and set the theme for the rest of their high school years.

Let's look at some case studies to make things more concrete. Mark currently attends the University of Pennsylvania. As a high school student, he was obviously a bright and motivated student but he didn't have any particularly outstanding skills; nor was he unusually brilliant. Now Mark knew from very early on that he wanted to be a business major. In the summer after his sophomore year, he applied for a position as a teller at a major bank and he continued to work this position year-round over the next two years, putting in ten to sixteen hours a week at this job while maintaining a solid GPA. What did this extracurricular activity demonstrate about Mark? It showed that Mark, a seemingly ordinary kid, possessed some remarkable qualities. First of all, he was reliable, well beyond the norm for a kid of his age. A major bank wouldn't employ anyone who was less than dependable. Second of all, Mark was extraordinarily persistent and consistent. He didn't just drop this activity when things got hectic at school. He spent a sizeable portion of his week on the job…and continued to do so for two solid years. Third of all, Mark had a great ability to juggle schoolwork and a real job. In a nutshell: Mark showed character.

One thing to take away from this case study is that an extraordinary extracurricular activity doesn't depend on having extraordinary talents. Let's face it. There are only so many Tiger Woodses and Mark Zuckerbergs walking around in the world. Fortunately, though, an extracurricular activity can be extraordinary because it displays an extraordinarily well-developed and admirable character. And although we can't create talent where there is none, we can certainly foster character.

Another thing to note from this case study is that Mark wouldn't have had the *option* of pursuing this one activity for such a long and impressive period of time if he hadn't started early enough. Students should really make sure to use the summers after their sophomore years wisely. Of course Mark knew what he wanted to do from really early on, and he never changed his mind. Students who aren't quite as sure about things as Mark should still make sure to spend the summer trying something new, something challenging.

Now let's consider, what could a student like Mark add on to his extracurricular activities his junior year to build on his profile? Taking a business elective would be a good idea. So would participating in the Future Business Leaders of America (FBLA), either taking up a leadership position in the club or founding a branch if the club doesn't already exist.

Let's look at another case study. June was very interested in journalism. She attended a high school with a really stellar, award-winning school newspaper. Becoming an editor at this newspaper is big news: it's a much-coveted position and colleges know it! For June to be a serious contender for the position of editor-in-chief her *senior* year, she had to start strategizing *as a sophomore*. She had to start acting like a leader from very early on: she had to be willing to take on additional responsibilities; she had to be bold enough to float new ideas; she had to get to know faculty advisors and seek to learn from current editors.

Now if June had attended a high school where the journalism program wasn't as competitive, she wouldn't have needed to get started so early or pursue things so aggressively. However, in that case, she also shouldn't have satisfied herself with scoring a readily available and inconsequential position. A student with true initiative would create opportunities in a situation like this.

Another student I counseled, Danielle, did just this. Not satisfied with the caliber of her school newspaper—or with the caliber of her school in general—she founded a quarterly magazine with a political tilt where students could explore and express their views. At the same time, she lobbied her school to add more AP courses to the curriculum. Though she found herself in a mediocre school with limited offerings, Danielle proved herself to be a true leader. She left behind a concrete legacy when she matriculated at Harvard.

These are just a few examples of students who made good use of their sophomore years. For sophomores reading this now, I'd advise them to be optimistic! Students who are open to figuring out what they're really good at and what they really love will have a better chance of finding their talents and passions!

4.7 Advice for Juniors

Here's the bad news for current juniors: it is not the best time to start thinking about extracurricular activities. One of the main things that colleges look for in a student is consistency and commitment. A sudden passion developed late junior year, say, for the welfare of baby seals, will probably not ring true. "What admissions officers look for is an elusive characteristic called integration," says Cigus Vanni, who worked in the admissions office of Swarthmore College. "'You look at the whole. Do all these parts fit together? You can tell if kids are doing this to pad the résumé or because someone told them to do it."[59]

What does this mean for the junior who hasn't really rolled up her sleeves yet? The junior without any real activities, let alone an outstanding activity? Such students shouldn't throw in the towel yet! Those who use their summer wisely can still make a material difference to their admissions chances. They can still do things now to maximize their chances of getting accepted at their dream college.

But a lot depends on exactly when a junior decides to get serious. Let's look at the case of Charles. Charles came to us at the end of his junior year. He had all the right numbers: straight As in his school's IB program; 4s and 5s on all his APs; and a solid SAT score of 2100. With numbers like these, he was a strong candidate for the upper-level UCs. But Charles interested in attending a private college. In particular, he really wanted to study pre-med at Johns Hopkins University. Unfortunately, he had prioritized studying at the expense of everything else over the last few years. He had spent all his time studying, and so far he had nothing else to show. The only

---

[59] Nussbaum, Debra. "It's Time to Polish Résumés." *New York Times*. 25 May 2003.

extracurricular activity he'd participated in was the school tennis team. Although he had played since freshman year, he wasn't even a standout tennis player. What should Charles have done?

Well, here's one thing Charles should *not* have done: quit tennis. Senior year is not the time to be cutting back on commitments. But in addition, it was important for Charles to think of activities linked to tennis—his sole constant extracurricular—that could serve to highlight other aspects of his personality. For example, I suggested that Charles might recruit some teammates to create a group that teaches tennis to underprivileged children in the neighboring vicinities.

What else could Charles do? I urged Charles to think very hard about how he was going to spend the one precious summer he still had available to him. He had to search for a distinguishing activity that could generate a compelling college essay...and maybe even a recommendation letter. Given Charles's aspirations, I suggested he try to secure a medical mission trip to a foreign country. This would surely supply him with some great stories to turn into a college essay; it could also have garnered him a recommendation from a doctor. Alternatively, I suggested that Charles seek out a research opportunity or an internship. There are lots of prestigious summer internships with competitive application processes, but students who have missed deadlines or who, like Charles, could benefit from going the extra mile might try and procure an internship opportunity that *isn't* widely available to any high school student. Contacting professors or medical doctors—though only after doing due diligence and getting to know what the professors are researching or what the doctors are specializing in—can result in a one-of-a-kind opportunity and display initiative. One student I counseled was able to get herself a spot at a UC Irvine research program that is usually reserved for college students; she is currently attending the University of Pennsylvania.

Now let's compare Claire to Charles. Claire came to us early in her junior year with an academic profile much like Charles. But where Charles's main activity was tennis, Claire's was band.

Band, in and of itself, took up a whole lot of Claire's first two years of high school. But after learning about the college admissions process, Claire realized—still early in her junior year—that she had to differentiate herself from her band-mates. Claire figured out how to do this with a lot of imagination and dedication. In one year of hard work, Claire mobilized a team of her band-mates to go to a local community outreach organization and teach kids how to play instruments. She raised money to procure instruments for these children, and she got them practicing and excited about music. Then she organized a community concert to let the kids showcase their newfound abilities. Over the summer, Claire generated more buzz about the program; she even got the city mayor to attend one of the children's concerts! What was so impressive about Claire was that she found a way to take an interest she already had—a passion for music—and use it as a springboard for other activities. Her extracurricular profile ended up having breadth, depth, and narrative continuity. It certainly impressed Yale.

The most important thing I want to emphasize to juniors is that it's not yet too late…but it's *almost* too late. Students who accomplish a lot the crucial summer before senior year will make themselves more competitive applicants, regardless of how much they've accomplished so far.

4.8 Advice for Seniors

Senior year affords students some new opportunities. Cream-of-the-crop leadership positions are usually reserved for seniors. Plus, students who turn eighteen become eligible for a whole new range of volunteer positions and jobs.

It is important for seniors to make sure that they continue pursuing some of the activities they have developed thus far in order to show consistency and continuity. This is one case in which I sometimes advise students to participate in extracurricular activities that they downright don't want to do anymore. Students who have attained all but their Eagle Scout badge, for example, or who have practiced tae-kwon-do from when they were little kids all the way through junior year—such students should seriously consider continuing to participate in these activities their senior year whether they want to or not.

It is also very important that seniors not pack up their activities once their applications are in the mail. They should bear in mind that if they are wait-listed, they will be invited to send updates of their latest grades and extracurricular achievements to colleges. A stellar extracurricular project might help a student get off the wait-list.

(Anecdotally, this seems much more likely when a student is wait-listed at a smaller liberal arts college than when the student is one of thousands wait-listed at a school like Duke University. Larger research universities often use the wait list as a way to balance their incoming class with that last necessary violist or a handful of linguistics majors—and there's little a student can do to materially affect this calculation.)

The last several sections offered advice specifically targeted at students at different stages of their high school careers. In the next section, I'll present two real-life case studies. A detailed analysis of these two students should help bring together and illustrate several of the themes explored above in a concrete way.

4.9 A Comparative Case Study

Eric and Julie were two students I counseled through the Fall 2010 application cycle. Both applied early to Harvard and had stellar academics, outstanding extracurricular activities, and strong recommendations to back up their applications. To the casual observer, both seemed like a shoo-in, even at the most prestigious school in the U.S. However, only one of these students got in. Let's see who got in and why.

Let me warn students again not to use any of these case studies as a blueprint on which to model their own extracurricular records! No two students are alike. If students and their parents take just one message away from this chapter, it should be to discover and nurture genuine passions...and colleges will respond.

Student 1: Eric

Eric's academic profile

SAT: 2360

SAT Subject Tests:
800 on four tests

APs: 5 on seven tests

9th-grade GPA:
Straight As

10th-grade GPA (two APs):
Straight As

11th-grade GPA (five APs):
Straight As

Highlights of Eric's
extracurricular profile

**Neuroscience Internship
at Stanford University:**
40 hours a week the summer
before senior year

Science Olympiad:
National Semifinalist

Model United Nations (MUN) Club:
President

Speech and Debate:
Co-captain

Student 2: Julie

Julie's academic profile

SAT: 2370

SAT Subject Tests:
800 on three tests;
740 on two additional tests

APs:
5 on four tests; 4 on one test

9th-grade GPA:
Straight As

10th-grade GPA (one AP):
Straight As *except*
one B+ second semester

11th-grade GPA (five APs):
Straight As *except*
one B+ each semester

Highlights of Julie's
extracurricular profile

School Newspaper: Editor-in-Chief

YWCA: Student Representative on the
Board of Directors;
founder of a YWCA newsletter

OC Register: Summer Intern

**National Organization for Women
(NOW) Club:** President

Navy Junior ROTC: Section Captain

Colt Award for Poetry: First Prize

Analysis

First of all, both of these students did an incredible job throughout high school and should be commended for their efforts. Neither student did anything wrong. However, as I already gave away, one of these students was accepted early to Harvard and the other was straight-up rejected, not even deferred. Let's analyze each student's profile to better under-stand what Harvard saw.

Eric's academic record was perfect. He took the maximum number of APs available at his school and earned straight As in class and perfect 5s on the AP exams. His SAT scores were all achieved on the first attempt and he was expected to graduate as valedictorian.

Julie's academic record was also very strong, although not quite as impeccable as Eric's. Though she earned a few B+s, she too took the maximum number of APs available at her school and did almost perfectly on her six AP tests. Her SAT scores were also all achieved on the first try.

Eric's extracurricular profile confirmed the story told by his academic record. He was a very bright student who was well prepared for college level work. Summer research programs require intellectual curiosity, and the Stanford Neuroscience summer internship for high school students is one of the most competitive opportunities around. The fact that Eric was a Science Olympiad Semifinalist also attested to his intellectual ability. And his participation in MUN and Speech & Debate displayed academic well-roundedness.

Julie's extracurricular profile was also very strong. Her personal interest and talent in writing was attested to by her position as Editor-in-Chief of her school newspaper and by her poetry prize. Julie's activities also gave colleges a good glimpse of who she was and how she would contribute to the college community. Her involvement in the NOW Club and the YWCA displayed her interest in women's issues. She also took initiative in starting a newsletter for the YWCA, and her work was recognized by her appointment as the first student representative to the YWCA Board of Directors. Lastly, her involvement in NJROTC said a lot about her character and her values.

By now, readers may have guessed that Julie earned early admission to Harvard while Eric did not. Though Eric's profile revealed his academic preparedness and his ability to succeed at the highest levels intellectually, he did a poor job of showing his personality and his extra-academic values. Julie, on the other hand, revealed more than a set of intellectual talents. She communicated her character and showed how she would fit into college life. Although she received a few Bs, she remained well within the range considered academically qualified—even at a school like Harvard. And her stellar extracurricular profile sealed the deal. Although we rightly expected that Eric would be admitted to almost every college he applied to, at Harvard, he fell a bit short.

4.10 Last Words of Advice for Parents

This chapter opened with an exercise aimed at parents. I'll bookend the chapter with another section directed at parents.

All parents want what's best for their children. Thinking about colleges and extracurricular activities is obviously stressful, but I want to encourage parents to view this process as an opportunity to help their children discover their true interests and abilities. At the end of the day, extracurricular activities should simply reflect a student's passions.

As a professional résumé reader, I find it very easy to identify students who genuinely love what they do and students who are just looking for something to put on their applications. How? First of all, students who truly enjoy what they're doing *make* time—even amidst incredibly demanding schedules—to do that very thing. Another thing: students who love what they do see it through to the end. They don't start things and then quit just when school gets difficult or finals roll around. Students who quit a project reveal that they weren't all that passionate about it to begin with. The student who really loves to play water-polo *will* wake up every morning to practice water-polo. The student who loves to write *will* stay up all night putting the finishing touches on a poem or short story. In other words, extracurricular activities should not be a chore—and correctly chosen, they *won't* be a chore.

Now colleges make a big deal out of extracurricular activities because they genuinely want to see the true colors and individuality of each applicant. Helping a student find his or her true passion is one of the greatest gifts parents can give …and one of the best ways they can help the student get into a great college.

When I offer this counsel to families, many parents says that their student hasn't really demonstrated any particular interest or passion. Now I believe that it's the parents' job to put students in various environments where they can identify their passions.

Parents should start by using their student's school as a resource. They could get a comprehensive list of all the clubs and activities offered at school. Chances are, there are lots of opportunities parents have never even heard about.

Parents can also seek out professional counseling services, such as those offered at FLEX. Counselors have access to a lot of information that isn't so readily available. But more importantly, counselors have a lot of experience: they've seen lots of students who get in…and lots of students who don't. This broad picture is crucial to putting a particular student's achievements in perspective.

Parents should also be willing to send children out of their comfort zone. If a student qualifies for a gifted program such as the Johns Hopkins University Center for Talented Youth (CTY) or Stanford Educational Program for Gifted Youth (EPGY), the student should go! Many very selective universities (including, for example, the University of Pennsylvania, Cornell and the University of Chicago) also run their own summer programs for high school students. Admission into these programs, which usually run from three to six weeks, is not nearly as competitive as admission to the university. Participation in such programs is meant to demonstrate intellectual curiosity, rather than academic prowess. After all, colleges love students who love to learn.

A quick side note for parents reluctant to send their children away from home: some colleges are less likely to accept students applying from far-off regions because they recognize that families often turn out to be unwilling to send their children so far away. West Coast parents thinking about sending their children to an East Coast school might want to demonstrate the seriousness of their intent by sending students to distant summer programs or taking students on campus visits before the application process.

This bring me to travel: another invaluable experience, whether a student heads to Spain with his or her Spanish class or simply takes part in a field trip to Washington D.C. Travel is a cultural education in and of itself. It expands a student's worldview and provides some of that broader perspective that colleges value. As I mentioned above, colleges like students to have some sense of the world beyond their familiar hometowns. They want students who are going to bring an awareness of what's going on both locally and globally, as well as a willingness to act on that knowledge.

In closing, I want to emphasize that the value of extracurricular activities doesn't just lie in the achievement itself. What do I mean? First of all, admissions officers know that participating in extracurricular activities develops social and intellectual abilities, regardless of whether students win awards or take high profile leadership positions. Participating in Speech and Debate, for example, fosters the ability to think analytically and critically, skills necessary for success in college. Participating in Model U.N. trains students to partake in a dialogue and reach for a broader perspective. Both clubs develop a student's ability to do research.

Second of all, college admissions officers recognize that consistent participation in extracurricular activities takes—and develops—character. Ongoing commitment displays maturity, dependability and the ability to juggle many competing demands: skills that are necessary if students are going to succeed at the more selective universities.

Finally, I emphasize again that exceptional extracurricular records don't depend on exceptional talents or skills. Of course, the academic, athletic and musical superstars will always have a place at the most selective universities, and students with rare talents should by all means be given every opportunity to develop their gifts. But the vast majority of students who get accepted do not possess some rarified talent. They are just those who are able to maximize the abilities they have for some greater good. A pianist can be exceptional not because of his exceptional talent, but because his huge heart motivated lots of other musicians to join him in providing free weekly lessons to underprivileged students. An aspiring biologist can be a stand-out applicant not because of her participation in cutting-edge research, but because her environmental passion drove her to organize a community recycling program.

In closing, I remind parents that there is no one right course of action for everyone. Parents who really want to help their students develop their extracurricular profiles should think about this task as an opportunity for students to get to know themselves better and discover their real talents and passions. Many students will take some missteps; some students will need a gentle shove; every student will need encouragement. But the experience in and of itself can end up being invaluable.

Chapter 5: Essays, Recommendations & Interviews

Students who have built up solid GPAs, posted strong standardized test scores, and invested time and energy to develop extracurricular activities that they are passionate about have done most of the hard work...but they're not quite finished yet! Students must still take the final step and *present* themselves truthfully but compellingly in their college applications. The college essay, recommendations and interview are crucial framing devices that contextualize a student's achievements, focus attention on his or her strengths and add personality and three-dimensionality to a list of achievements.

In this chapter, I'll explain how to write a stellar college essay (also called the personal statement). While most of these recommendations are obviously directed at rising seniors, students at earlier stages of their high school careers should still pay attention, since it's never too early to be on the lookout for the activities and experiences that can inspire a powerful college essay. I'll also provide tips for lining up strong recommendations and nailing the college interview.

5.1 Is the College Essay (Really That) Important?

Every year, as summer vacations wind down, rising seniors hit that rite of passage: college essay season. All across the country, sixteen- and seventeen-year-olds struggle to find the five-hundred words that capture their unique identity and personality and help them stand out from tens of thousands of competing college applicants. One parent reflected on this in the *New York Times.* Sitting through dozens of informational sessions with admissions deans, this parent heard over and over how important the personal essay is—how it "is the one element where a student's own voice can be heard through the fog of quantitative data." But, as the parent noted, "Prose in which an author's voice emerges...is the hardest kind of writing there is. Plenty of professional authors can't manage it. How reasonable is it to expect of teenagers?"[60] Unsurprisingly, this task, which would flummox most adults, can reduce even the most levelheaded high school student to a state of high panic. In fact, I've heard a student say that he was "lucky" to be the victim of a cruel act of racism because it gave him something unique to write about.

The next few sections of this book are devoted to clearing up some widespread misperceptions about the college essay and to providing concrete, usable strategies for writing a compelling essay. Too many students waste the real opportunity they have here. Many just aren't even sure how much weight the essay "really" carries in the admissions process. So I'll start by answering this fundamental question. Just how important *is* the college essay?

There are six elements that factor into private college admissions. In order of importance, they are GPA, standardized test scores (SATs or ACT), extracurricular activities, personal essay, recommendations and interview. Note that the college

---

[60] Gabriel, Trip. "The Almighty Essay." *New York Times.* 07 Jan 2011.

essay is the fourth most important factor, coming right after a student's academic profile and extracurricular activities. Students hoping to be competitive at the most selective schools—schools such as the Ivies and Stanford—*cannot afford to drop the ball on any one of these six factors.* While a spectacular essay *alone* cannot make up for a lackluster transcript or an indifferent extracurricular record, it can be *the* factor that selects between two students with similar academic statistics and comparable levels of extracurricular accomplishment. And remember, the vast majority of students who gain entrance into a school like Stanford have uniformly high, practically perfect levels of academic accomplishment. Barmak Nassirian, Associate Director of the American Association of Collegiate Registrars and Admissions Officers, starkly illustrates the importance of the college essay. "Admissions officers are running out of calibration devices," he told the *New York Times.* "All else being the same or similar, the essay suddenly becomes…a tie breaker."[61]

So is the college essay (really that) important? Yes. It is *that* important, especially for private colleges. In fact, in the last analysis, the college essay can be *the* factor that gets one candidate in and keeps another out.

5.2 Writing the College Essay: Dos and Don'ts

Most importantly: students should be themselves

To get started, I want to emphasize that students should look upon the college essay as a unique opportunity. It's a chance for the writer to reveal something about him- or herself *that cannot be found anywhere else in the application.* Robin Mamlet, Dean of Admissions at highly exclusive Swarthmore College, has been reading college essays for sixteen years. He says that when he looks at an essay, "it's not with a thought of, 'Is the student going

---

[61] Gabriel, Trip. "The Almighty Essay." *New York Times.* 07 Jan 2011.

to dazzle me?' Or 'Is the student going to make me laugh?'" The real question, Mamlet says, is, "Who is this person?"[62] College essays are supposed to be *personal* statements—and admissions officers are truly interested in just that. They want to get to know applicants as three-dimensional people: they want to see the personality behind the grades; they want to hear the voice behind the activities. So the best thing students can do in their college essays is to be themselves, not whatever persona they think college admissions officers want.

Students should package themselves

However, students do want to present themselves in the best possible light. That is, students want to package themselves. The student receiving Cs in history class who doesn't have any extracurricular activities with a historical focus probably doesn't want to write an essay about his or her love of history! As much as possible, the essay should complement the other aspects of a student's application. A good essay will bind together a student's academic and extracurricular profile and help present the applicant in a unified way.

Students should sound like themselves

Students also want to sound like themselves…without being inappropriately casual. This is a tricky balance to strike. The personal statement should be more casual in tone than essays written for school. This is not the place for students to show-off their hard-earned SAT vocabulary!

However, students must also treat their readers with due respect and seriousness. College admissions officers shouldn't be treated like a best friend or confidante. A certain level of professionalism is still expected.

---

[62] Goldberg, Carey. "Admissions Essay Ordeal: The Young Examined Life." *New York Times.* 31 Dec 1997.

Students should tell a story

Finally—and this one is key—students should *tell a story.* In fact, students should stop thinking about the personal statement as an "essay" or even a "statement." Essays and statements are serious things, often pretty tough-going: hard to write and hard to read. Students should rather think of finding and telling a story. People like to read stories. Stories invite people in; they're fun, even exciting, to read. And everyone intuitively knows what makes a good story.

Two don'ts

Now there are some common but costly mistakes that students make when writing their college essay. And all too often, these mistakes arise because there is a real disconnect between what admissions officers are looking for and what students *think* admissions officers are looking for.

The most common mistake I see is the brag sheet-as-college essay. Students who try to impress their reader with a full account of their achievements and accolades are wasting their time. *All that information can be found elsewhere in the application.* These students are just taking all the details they've provided in succinct and highly readable list form…and repeating it in long-winded paragraph form! In the best case scenario, these essays are a wasted opportunity, since admissions officers are left with no new information. In the worst case scenario, these essays turn out to be a real chore to read. And students don't want to alienate admissions officers who can determine their fate!

Students should also avoid the other extreme, however. As I already mentioned, the admissions officer is not a friend; nor is he or she a therapist. Students should stay away from sob stories, overly casual language, or gimmicks meant to attract the attention of the admissions committee. (One student wrote a compelling essay on fishing…but ended up sending an admissions officer to the emergency room when the fishing hook he attached to the essay quite *literally* hooked his reader right through the hand.[63]) Students should also use a measure of common sense in deciding what to share and what not to share. For example, one student wanted to write an essay about how bored he was with a class in order to explain a C that didn't even show up on his official transcript. Bad move! Another student joked about how she wanted to go to a school close to home so that her mom could continue to do her laundry. Students should make sure their college essays are memorable *in a good way.*

In the next two sections, I'll present two student profiles and explain how these applicants should and shouldn't approach their personal statements. We'll think about which topics would work and which wouldn't, and I'll show what the college essay looks like from the standpoint of the bleary-eyed, over-worked college admissions officer.

5.3 Case Study: Joan, the Exceptional Student with the Average Essay

Meet Joan. Many would call Joan the "perfect daughter." Born to a career diplomat, Joan never lived in one location for any length of time. She was born in Korea, grew up in Brazil, returned to Korea for the last year of middle school and then immigrated to the U.S. to finish up high school in southern California. Joan's itinerant childhood bred in her an informed interest in international relations and politics, and this is what she hoped to major in. Joan took full advantage of the related extracurricular activities available to her, immersing herself in Model U.N. and picking up a total of five foreign languages. Finally, Joan genuinely loved learning, and this clearly showed in her transcript. She consistently excelled despite taking an ambitious course load filled with advanced courses, and she received high standardized test scores.

---

[63] Marcus, Dave. "Not the 'Hook' the Admissions Office Had in Mind." *New York Times.* 29 Oct 2010.

The details of Joan's application profile are given on the next page. Obviously, Joan did all the hard work necessary to get into a top private school. In fact, she looked perfectly positioned to get into an Ivy League university. She applied to all the Ivy League schools, some of the top smaller liberal arts colleges and a few other high-ranking private schools, including Stanford. She was rejected by every single one. Today, she is at UC Berkeley. Getting into Berkeley is, of course, a great achievement in and of itself. However, the question still remains. Why didn't Joan get in? What could she possibly have done wrong?

Well, there was only one weakness in Joan's application: her college essay. Joan wrote a typical "immigration" essay in which she discussed the hardships she experienced after moving to the U.S. as a high school student. She talked about how she was able to overcome the language barrier through determination and hard work. Now there is nothing *wrong* with this essay topic, but there is also nothing interesting about it either. This essay could have been written by any one of the tens of thousands of immigrants applying to college every year. (In fact, this essay *is* written by tens of thousands of these students every year!)

Joan's essay failed to touch on any one of the many things unique to *Joan*. It didn't give any specifics, for example, of her time in Brazil, or talk about what it was like to move around so frequently as a child. Joan's essay also didn't mention her extensive extracurricular activities at all. It didn't explain *why* Joan was motivated to participate in those particular activities. All in all, Joan's essay didn't provide readers with any answer to the question, Why this particular applicant over all the others?

Joan's academic profile:

SAT: 2280

SAT Subject Tests:
700+ on three tests

APs: All 4s and 5s

9th-grade GPA: Straight As

10th-grade GPA: Straight As

11th-grade GPA (five APs):
Straight As except one B

12th-grade GPA (five APs):
Straight As

Foreign-language skills:
Fluent in Korean, English,
Spanish and Portuguese;
proficient in Japanese

Highlights of Joan's
extracurricular profile:

Speech and Debate: Captain
(junior and senior year)

World Affairs Council:
Participant (three years)

Band: Principal clarinetist;
member (four years)

**Four-week Summer Environmental
Research Internship at UCLA**

Student Council: Secretary

Now in the previous section, I offered some pointers for writing a strong personal statement. Students, I said, should be themselves, only tidily packaged up. They should sound like their best selves as they tell a personal story about themselves.

Where did Joan's essay go wrong? Joan failed to package herself attractively. And she didn't even try to tell a story. Let's start with the second mistake.

Joan was a student who had been exposed to multiple cultures from a very young age. Her essay should not have begun when Joan moved to the U.S. from Korea. That story is an old, familiar, and often tired one. Joan's essay should have started instead with her experiences in Brazil. Joan didn't attend an international school in Brazil. Rather, she attended a small Brazilian school as the only Asian student. A brief anecdote about her experiences in the Brazilian elementary school could very easily have caught a reader's attention. Or Joan could have talked about how, just as she was getting acclimated to Brazilian culture, her father's job took her back to Korea, where she entered the famously intense and radically different Korean educational system, without having the same academic background and training as her peers. Against such a backdrop, Joan's coming-to-America story could suddenly look very different and very new.

Now let's turn to the other mistake Joan made in her college essay: her failure to package herself. Joan was most definitely not a passive kid. She *used* her multicultural experiences: they inspired her to learn several languages and get involved in projects with a global dimension. But none of this information emerged in her college essay. She wasn't able to show how her life story informed her choices and gave rise to specific intellectual interests. She didn't use her essay to show how her different activities and academic accomplishments cohered with each other and informed each other. Joan's stereotypical "coming to America" essay portrayed her as just another immigrant. So although Joan did all the hard work, her failure to package herself well kept her from being a compelling applicant.

A better essay would have allowed readers to see Joan as a student who had faced quite serious and unusual challenges from a much earlier age, but who faced these challenges head-on, turning them into advantages and refusing to be a passive bystander in her life.

Of course, not everyone has a story like Joan's to tell. Students who do not have particularly unique backgrounds should not feel that this puts them at a disadvantage in the application process. They might have to look a bit harder to find their story, but every student has some story that only he or she can tell. The next case study shows how one student from a very "normal" background met this challenge.

5.4 Case Study: Sam, the Average Student with the Great Essay

Sam was a multi-tasking, over-achieving student from a reputable public school in the Bay Area. An Asian-American student from a relatively affluent background, he was, on the face of it, very similar to many of his peers. Like most of his classmates, Sam took difficult classes, got pretty good grades, and achieved solid standardized test scores.

Now Sam's profile seems really common. What story could he tell that his peers couldn't? But of course, everyone's life history *is* unique. Compelling college essays don't have to emerge from uncommon experiences or unusual activities. Some of the best emerge from finding what's special in seemingly everyday experiences, apparently ordinary lives. This is something Sam did exceptionally well.

Let's look at the details of Sam's academic profile and then see how he approached his college essay.

Sam's academic profile:

SAT: 2180

SAT Subject Tests:
600+ on three

APs: All 4s and 5s

9th-grade GPA: Straight As

10th-grade GPA: Straight As

11th-grade GPA (three APs):
Straight As

12th-grade GPA (four APs):
Straight As except for one B

Highlights of Sam's
extracurricular profile:

Marching Band: President
(junior and senior year)

Church Youth Group: Participant
(four years)

Environmental Club: Participant
(four years)

Spanish Club: President

On paper, Sam had a very standard, unexceptional but solid extracurricular record. On his first try at his college essay, he came up with a draft that was also solid but unexceptional. Here's an excerpt from this first draft, written about his experience playing trumpet in marching band:

> *Walking down through the dark entrance into the field, it was like entering the Coliseum as a gladiator. I could feel the adrenaline rush through the veins of my body, my heart race, and my ears get hotter. I set up, did my*

microphone check, and ran to my first set in the field show. Ready. Set. Go! The show started and I began the art of multi-tasking required in marching: count my steps, play my music, march with precise technique, keep my trumpet up parallel to the ground, and constantly adjust my position in relation to my marching peers.

Now there is nothing *wrong* with this. However, it could have been written by any of the other musicians in Sam's marching band or, for that matter, by any student participating in any of the marching bands across the U.S. What the reader doesn't get from this excerpt is a sense of the extent to which *Sam* was really invested in marching band. As a result, this essay did Sam a disservice. It didn't highlight what was really unique about him.

Here's some more relevant information about Sam. Sam was president of his marching band for two years. His role wasn't limited to showing up for practice sessions and performances. Rather, Sam took an uninspired team which had lost two directors in two years and turned it into a strong, invigorating competitor that made it to the California state semifinals. In addition, Sam was able to revive the band festival: an event that used to be held annually at his school but had been canceled in recent years. Under Sam's leadership, this tradition was resurrected, and Sam's senior year, his school hosted thirty area bands over two days of competition and performances. This feat attracted the notice of the district supervisor. Lastly, Sam showed character in the little things as well as the big. He was the first to arrive and the last to leave every fundraiser, practice session, and performance. This did not go unnoticed by the band director who, unsurprisingly, wrote one of Sam's recommendations.

Although playing in a marching band is a very common activity, Sam's band experience was obviously highly unique. He wasn't just another participant. This came out clearly in Sam's second attempt at writing his essay. Here is an excerpt:

6:00 PM. I have not been home for more than an hour and I'm on my way back. I have to be at the school gym to set up a stage. This is easier said than done. The members of the stage crew filter in. It takes all five of us to carry the tarp from the storage closet and roll it across the vast gym floors. We wrestle the concert acoustic shells—each at least twice as tall as we are—into position. Then we start to move chairs; hundreds of chairs; chairs from classrooms all over the school. We are setting the stage for our school's annual Band Festival to be held here the next day.

My high school has traditionally hosted an instrumental music festival every year. Over a period of two days, thirty bands and hundreds of band members descend on our high school in the spirit of friendly competition. This event had not been held for the last two years because it was such a logistical hassle to pull off. Then, in 2006, I became band president and our new director decided to "challenge me," as he put it. I had no idea what this challenge entailed. But in finding out the hard way, I discovered talents I didn't know I had.

This essay works on many levels. It engages the reader's interest. It has narrative flow, and all the specific details plunge readers into a textured, colorful world. Readers also get a sense of the author's unique personality: we *see* Sam's determination, his willingness to take on a challenge, his dedication, without being *told* any of this explicitly. In short, this essay does everything that a college essay should do.

Now Sam, armed with this great essay, was able to gain admission to some of the most selective colleges in the U.S. Although he was rejected at the University of Chicago, Dartmouth, Duke and Stanford, he was accepted at Brown, Cornell, Northwestern and Washington University in St Louis. Notice how easily Sam's extracurricular résumé could have looked ordinary. If he merely listed "President of Marching Band" under his activities, colleges would never have been able to appreciate the depth of commitment and quality of leadership that Sam really did demonstrate. Sam's essay was the crucial bit of packaging that helped him stand out and get in.

5.5 Writing the "Why X College" Essay

The previous two sections focused on the personal statement: the main college essay. However, lots of colleges ask other supplementary questions. One of the most straightforward but still difficult questions students see on a college application is the Why us? question. Why Stanford? Why Princeton University's College of Engineering?

This question is obviously harder to answer for students who haven't had the opportunity to visit a college and experience it firsthand. And it's impossible to answer adequately without doing some research. But there are pitfalls that will trip up even those students who have done due diligence and know what they're talking about.

Let's look at one common mistake. One student essay I read said the following:

> *There isn't a particular person who prompted my interest in Brown. While we were touring schools, my dad announced that our next stop was "Brown." However, after visiting the campus and meeting its students, I discovered the vibrancy and brilliance that give Brown an unmistakable identity.*

There is little to object to about the writing itself. This student has obviously carefully crafted these sentences, thinking hard about word choice, phrasing, flow, etc. The problem lies in *what* is being said. Any student can talk about the "vibrancy and brilliance" of Brown—even the student who knows nothing about Brown except that it's a well-known school! This essay utterly fails to explain why Brown is a great fit for this particular student. The next excerpt succeeds where the first failed:

'Comparative Health Systems: Hong Kong,' taught by Professor Kagan, merges my work at the San Francisco Department of Public Health with my love for the city of Hong Kong. I've been able to actively compare the two systems during my internship. While working in the San Francisco Department of Public Health the summer before my senior year, I wrote a basic lesson plan on nutrition to teach at an English summer camp in Guangdong Province, China. There, I experienced firsthand the differences between the knowledge of the students in China and the knowledge of the students in California.

This was written by a student applying to the University of Pennsylvania. Notice how the student used his own personal experiences and academic interests to explain why he was interested *specifically in U Penn*. He was able to point admissions officers to the specifics of his own profile without straying away from the scope of the "Why U Penn" question. Also, by referring to Professor Kagan's class, this student showed that he had done quite a bit of research about U Penn. He had obviously read through the course catalog, envisioned himself at U Penn and thought about which of the many concrete opportunities that only U Penn has to offer he'd most want to take advantage of. This student had thought *seriously* about where to go to college. His decision wasn't based just on the name value of the school; he had deep-seated reasons to apply to U Penn, which made it likely that he'd accept an offer of admission if it were made.

A note of warning. The particular tactic of naming one specific course is catching on and becoming rather too common. It's certainly not the right approach for everyone, although it might still be the right approach for some. The best thing for students to do is not to worry too much about fads, but also not to model their answers on anyone else's. Students should visualize themselves at the university, pretend they get to select courses or join in activities or explore the surrounding city, and see what truly captures their imagination.

5.6 Teacher Recommendations

Recommendations are the only *personal* yet *third-party* perspectives colleges get on a candidate. They function as an independent validation of what the student has said about himself or herself; they can also help shed light on the student's circumstances, both personal (family problems, for example) and general (how challenging the school generally is; what opportunities were unavailable).

Note: the UCs don't require, and in fact won't accept, any recommendations. Because of this, California students are particularly unclear about the real purpose of recommendations, and should attend to the following information very carefully.

There are three types of recommendations: teacher, counselor and supplementary recommendations. Each has a different role to play. Most colleges require two teacher recommendations and one counselor recommendation. The supplementary recommendation is optional, and each school has its own policy for handling such letters. In this section, I'll be focusing on teacher recommendations.

It's pretty common knowledge among college counselors that the typical recommendation letter has very little influence on the fate of an applicant. Why? Because most letters are so identical they're interchangeable. In fact, Gerry Cox, a Dean of Admissions at Cornell, says he just sets aside generic letters when considering applicants. "The more they sound alike, the less difference they make," he says.[64]

However, a thoughtful recommendation letter from a writer who obviously really knows an applicant *can* make a difference. While

---

[64] Altschuler, Glenn. "College Prep: Dear Admissions Committee." *New York Times*. 09 Jan 2000.

such a letter won't get an *un*qualified student into a particular school, it can help distinguish one qualified applicant from a pile of similarly qualified applicants. What can a student do to maximize his or her chances of securing such a meaningful recommendation? Here are four general suggestions:

1. Students should get to know their teachers.

2. Students must plan ahead and be considerate to their recommenders.

3. Students should provide teachers with the information they need to write *personal* letters.

4. Students should waive the right to read their letters of recommendations.

Get to know teachers

One big problem that children from immigrant families particularly have is that they tend to be more quiet and passive in class and don't seek to establish relationships with adults. Now if a student gets an A in AP U.S. History but doesn't participate in class discussions, his or her teacher will probably write a good but generic recommendation about the student's academic achievement. Although the letter may contain many genuine compliments about the student's academic ability, this letter won't *add* any information to the student's profile, because the fact that this student was an able student who worked hard and did well in class would already be evident from the grade he or she received.

By comparison, the student with a B+ in AP U.S. History who, though not the smartest kid in the class, participated actively, went out of his way to help other students and asked thought-provoking questions of the teacher would be more likely to score a memorable recommendation.

The first student might receive a recommendation letter that says, "Sarah is an excellent student who performs well on all of her tests and essays. She is responsible about turning in her homework on time and is generally a high-achieving individual." The second student might receive a recommendation letter that says, "Noah was the spark that ignited classroom discussions, the student who read the whole book when only a chapter was assigned. His infectious enthusiasm for history motivated everyone around him to think a bit harder or re-think things once again." It should be obvious which recommendation would make a difference! The only way a student can get a recommendation like Noah's is by opening up and participating in class.

Plan ahead and be considerate

It is preferable for students to get recommendations from teachers of core academic subjects—math, for example, rather than photography. In addition, students should try to get recommendations from junior-year teachers: they're able to provide a more recent evaluation of student performance than sophomore-year teachers, but they also had a whole year to see the student in action, unlike senior-year teachers.

This means that rising juniors should start thinking about which instructors might be candidate letter-writers and seek to develop relationships with these teachers right from the beginning of the school year.

Rising seniors should download application materials as soon as they are available and get the recommendation forms to teachers in a timely and organized fashion. The little details really do matter. Students must remember that they are asking already busy instructors, who are most likely writing *dozens* of letters, to do them a favor. They must be sure to give teachers plenty of time to write the letter. They must also make sure their material is organized and neat: all sections that students fill out must be properly attended to and all forms should be accompanied by stamped and addressed envelopes. These little details can make a big difference to the teacher's perception of a student—and can subliminally affect how the teacher feels about the student! Finally, don't forget to send instructors a thank-you card when the process is over.

Provide information that the recommender can use to add concrete details and a personal touch

Teachers have many, many students. It can be difficult for a teacher to remember specific things about specific students, and it is perfectly appropriate for students to help teachers out with little reminders. Students might provide teachers with a copy of an essay that had received particularly outstanding comments, or with updates about extracurricular activities that have been motivated and informed by their classroom studies. These details can help a teacher write a more powerful and personal recommendation.

For example, here is an excerpt from one high school teacher's letter that really made an impact. Notice the specific details the teacher was able to recall:

> *Stefan used spirituals, sermons and slave narratives in an essay about dissimulation, double-entendre and psychological resistance among African-Americans before the Civil War. Deftly crafting his own interpretation of the slave personality, he was unafraid to challenge the assumptions of the distinguished scholars Stanley Elkins and Eugene Genovese. The result was one of the two finest papers in the junior class.*[65]

Stefan's history teacher was able to speak so convincingly about Stefan's academic abilities in large part because of the detailed discussion of Stefan's work. Obviously, Stefan's paper was really memorable! Stefan was accepted at Brown, despite having a comparatively weak GPA.

A word of warning: students must be sure to give teachers only select and relevant supplementary information. Teachers definitely do not appreciate being flooded with superfluous papers—this is extra work for them, after all!

---

[65] Altschuler, Glenn. "College Prep: Dear Admissions Committee." *New York Times*. 09 Jan 2000.

Waive the right to read recommendation letters

Students have the option to waive their right to read recommendation letters. They must make this decision *before* handing the recommendation forms to recommenders.

College admissions officers tend to give much less credit to letters that have been read by the applicant. Knowing a student might read the latter may very well impact the recommender's willingness to write in a completely candid fashion. Students who waive their right to read their recommendations demonstrate confidence in their relationship with the recommender.

In the ideal case, students should have no reason to doubt whether they will get solid recommendations. And most teachers will refuse to write a recommendation rather than write a poor one. However, when in doubt, a student can initiate a frank conversation and ask whether a teacher feels informed enough to write a strong recommendation.

5.7 Counselor and Supplementary Recommendations

Now let's turn to the other recommendations that complete a college application: the counselor recommendation and the optional supplementary recommendations.

The counselor recommendation

I said before that a recommendation is a *personal* but *third-party* perspective on a student that can provide independent validation of what the student says elsewhere on the application. To expand on this, I should point out that each recommendation type illuminates a different aspect of the student. Teacher recommendations attest to a student's ability in a particular subject area and his or her way of interacting intellectually with peers. School counselors, by contrast, see students in a broader context. In other words, a teacher will compare a student with other members of his or her *class* and will focus on the student's *academic* performance and character. A guidance counselor will compare a student with other members of his or her *grade* and factor in extracurricular activities and leadership roles as well as academic abilities.

However, the value of a counselor recommendation does not end with the bigger picture counselors provide. Here's a true story to think about. Lori Jacobson is a guidance counselor at a highly-respected public school in southern California. During her twenty-year tenure, she has seen handfuls of her students get into the most selective universities across the nation...year after year. Harvard University, for example, normally admits one or two students from Ms. Jacobson's school every year. Recently, Harvard initiated contact with Ms. Jacobson. The university had received applications from four very strong candidates in Ms. Jacobson's high school. Admissions officers had already decided to admit one, but they wanted Ms. Jacobson's help in choosing which of the three remaining candidates would get the second spot.

There are two things to take away from this story. First of all, students should not underestimate the amount of influence their guidance counselors have with colleges! Good guidance counselors can function as advocates for their student, initiating contact with college admissions offices and providing admissions committees with important information on behalf of their students.

Second of all, let's consider why Harvard University might enlist Ms. Jacobson's help. It must be because she can provide additional insight that cannot be found anywhere else, including in the applications themselves. What kind of information could a guidance counselor provide that a student can't? I already mentioned that guidance counselors can give crucial contextual information. They can tell a college how hard the AP Physics teacher really is and how many high-achieving students are too afraid to take the course. They can remind a college that their school Speech and Debate team is nationally-ranked and that captaining the team is a real honor.

There is another kind of information—information of a rather more personal kind—that is best heard from guidance counselors rather than from students themselves. One of the most important functions of a counselor recommendation is to detail any adversities and personal issues that might have affected a student's academic performance. Coming from a counselor, this kind of information amounts to an *explanation* of a weak term, for example, or a year of complete non-participation in extracurricular activities. Coming from the student directly, however, the same information inevitably sounds like an *excuse*, even if it's true.

Just last year, I worked with a student who was suffering from a rare eye disorder that required her to undergo multiple surgeries and skip school for a month. Now of course, the student was able to detail parts of her experience in her personal statement. But it was the counselor recommendation that really lent credibility to her application. The counselor was able to contextualize Diane's academic performance (straight As, 2100 SAT score) in light of her adversity. Diane's counselor could say what Diane couldn't: that her grades were all the more impressive because of the circumstances under which she achieved them. Ultimately, Diane, whose disability made her passionate about becoming a doctor, was admitted into a school with one of the top three medical programs in the nation: Washington University in St. Louis.

The case of Diane also points to something else a guidance counselor can do better than the student: brag. I already stressed that students shouldn't think of their essays as highlight reels. Rather, students should aim for modesty—and leave it to the cold hard numbers and the recommendations of others to do the rest.

The counselor recommendation is an invaluable and often neglected tool in the college admissions process. Although students need to be demure about their achievements and stoical about their hardships, counselors have no such constraints. In fact, their job is to boast about their students or to explain in full detail what hardships students have endured and overcome.

This means that it's critical for students to make a concerted effort to get to know their guidance counselors and keep them updated on their various activities. Students shouldn't just assume that counselors know what they're up to or what they're dealing with. One guidance counselor at a Bay Area private school had no idea that her student was a nationally recognized cellist since the student never told her! Students should make it a point to check in periodically with their guidance counselors. The more a counselor knows of a student's life, the more comprehensive a recommendation the counselor will be able to write.

The supplementary recommendation

The supplementary recommendation is an optional part of the application, and each school has its own policy for handling these letters. Here are a few guidelines to help a student decide whether or not to submit a supplementary letter of recommendation.

First of all, students must not be fooled into thinking that more is better or that more can't hurt. Students absolutely should *not* submit additional letters that say the same old thing and don't contribute anything to their profile. There is no quicker way to irritate a busy admissions officer than to send a whole bunch of unnecessary and repetitive information. (In fact, admissions officers have a saying: "the thicker the file, the thicker the applicant.")

Second of all, students shouldn't solicit recommendations from people who don't really know them. Students often try to get letters from school alumni, congressmen, celebrities, etc. However, a recommendation is only as valuable as the letter writer is knowledgeable! A student who gets a letter from a local congresswoman who knows nothing about the student will get a generic form letter.

Related to the last point: students shouldn't be narrow-minded in their idea of what makes a good recommender. Some of the best recommendation letters are written not by members of government or presidents of companies, but by people who really know a student in a different and revealing context. One Cornell admissions officer still remembers a recommendation he read several years ago. As he recalled it in an article for the *New York Times*, the recommendation had been written on behalf of "a young man from a comfortably middle-class family who had [been hired] as a manual laborer…. To the surprise of his boss, 'the kid' worked without complaint through stifling heat when several of the more experienced crew groused, took long lunches and asked to leave early." The admissions officer noted that he had seen "few letters address motivation more effectively" than this letter from a roofer. Unsurprisingly, the student was admitted.[66]

*   *   *

To summarize the last two sections, students shouldn't underestimate the importance of the recommendation letter. Although even an outstanding letter cannot compensate for other weaknesses in the application, it can make a material difference: it can explain why one student with a seemingly rock-solid application was rejected while another with near-identical numbers and activities was accepted.

Students should be realistic, however. The vast majority of letters end up being generically complimentary and therefore inconsequential. The best letters come from people with an intimate knowledge of the student. So instead of pinning hopes on chasing down big-name letter-writers or well-connected alumni, students should work on nurturing strong relationships with teachers who inspire them, guidance counselors who "get"

---

[66] Altschuler, Glenn. "College Prep: Dear Admissions Committee." *New York Times*. 09 Jan 2000.

them, and anyone else—bosses, internship coordinators, etc.—with whom they have meaningful contact.

5.8 The College Interview

I'll start the last section of this chapter with some cautionary tales. A few weeks ago, Nina, one of my counselees, was scheduled for an interview with her first-choice college, the University of Southern California (USC). At our next meeting, I asked Nina how the interview went. "Oh," she replied breezily, "it didn't." It turned out that Nina, feeling overwhelmed by schoolwork and application deadlines, had postponed the interview. "What did you tell the interviewer?" I asked. "The truth," she said, nonplussed. "I was too busy."

Nina's cavalier attitude is not all that uncommon. In fact, one interviewer for Harvard once had a student say, "This doesn't really count anyway," right in the middle of the interview![67]

Now it is true that the interview is the least important factor in a college application. However, it's a long way from "*least* important" to "*un*important." Students who confuse the two are making a very dangerous mistake.

Although there are many colleges that simply don't have the time or the resources to offer college interviews at all—the UC schools, for example—colleges that do offer interviews obviously consider them valuable. In fact, many schools still strongly recommend interviews (Yale, Princeton, Rice, plus many of the most selective liberal arts colleges). And a few still *require* them (most notably, Georgetown). Consider the following fact. Although Harvard doesn't require interviews, it turns out that, as Jeff Neal, spokesperson for the university puts it, "the vast

---

[67] Berman, Keith. "Preparing for the College Interview: An Insider's View." *Education Update Online*. Feb 2006. Web. 18 Feb 2011.

majority of students who are ultimately admitted to Harvard College have been interviewed."[68]

Although the interview is rarely *the* deciding factor in admission, it clearly provides important insight into an applicant's character. A stellar interview can result in a valuable letter of support: something like an extra letter of recommendation, but from someone who really knows the school and will have a concrete sense of how well the student would fit in with the school's values and culture.

So what in particular are schools looking for when they interview students? Interviewers are specifically asked to measure two things: a student's personality and his or her intellectual ability. Now although nobody can teach a student how to fake a sparkling personality or approximate a lightning-fast wit, we can tell students what *not* to do.

Let's return to the example set by Nina and see what kind of message her flippant postponement of her interview sent to USC. First of all, Nina apparently isn't very good at time management—she overbooked herself. Then, having over-extended herself, Nina decided to prioritize her personal needs. She placed greater value on her own to-do list than on the interviewer's time, disregarding the fact that the interviewer set aside a chunk of his or her own time to meet Nina. All in all, it's not looking like Nina particularly values or prioritizes USC: she just wasted it's time and resources. Nina made a bad impression before she even showed her face.

How can students avoid making a similar mistake? Below I'll list some of the most important things a student should *not* do during the college interview. Though what follows isn't a complete list of don'ts, it should help students avoid some of the worst mistakes.

---

[68] de Vise, Daniel. "How Important is the Admissions Interview?" *Washington Post.* 02 Aug 2010.

Don't arrive late!

In fact, students should arrive about ten minutes early. This is a way for the student to show that he or she appreciates the opportunity and values the interviewer's time.

Don't come underdressed.

It is far better to be overdressed than underdressed for the interview. A good rule of thumb is to wear "business casual" attire and leave the jeans for another day. In fact, in general, students should conduct themselves as though on a job interview. Relevant materials (résumé and portfolio, if necessary) should be neatly presented in a folder. Also, don't chew gum!

Don't bring mom or dad!

There should be no third party present during the interview. The interview is between student and interviewer. Students should prepare to be their own advocates.

Don't say too little…

Nothing kills an interview quicker than a series of mono-syllabic answers. Remember, the purpose of an interview question isn't necessarily to get a yes or no answer. A question might be intended to give interviewees the opportunity to provide further information. For example, an interviewer might say, "I see that you've participated in marching band for two years but dropped out last semester." This is not a request for interviewees to *confirm* information. It's an invitation for the student to explain *why* he or she was compelled to drop out.

…but don't say too much!

Let's return to the scenario above. Say John dropped out of marching band simply because he didn't *like* the new band director. In fact, he's not alone: pretty much no one liked the new band director, and rumor has it that this new guy was fired from his last job because of his inability to connect with students. All of this information might well be true, and John might have very good reasons to dislike the new band director. But the interview is *not* the place for unedited disclosure! There are some topics that are simply inappropriate for the interview. However affable the interviewer, he is not a friend...or a therapist.

Similarly, although I am by no means encouraging dishonesty, a little bit of self-editing is important. Everyone has stories of interviewees blurting interview-killers. "This is my back-up school." "I'm here because my parents made me come." "I want to go to Brown because I love Massachusetts." (FYI: Brown is in Rhode Island.)

Don't lie or exaggerate

This is actually a much more common problem than people might think. Half-truths can pop out, not because students intend to deceive interviewers, but simply because the student is nervous and out to impress! For example, a student might understandably answer a question like, "What is your favorite book?" by naming the most impressive title he or she can think of. But how is this student going to answer the natural follow-up question, "And what did you think of the famous battle scenes in *War and Peace*?"

In general, then, students shouldn't try to cater their answers to what they think the interviewer wants to hear. Such answers usually come off as unnatural and insincere.

Don't be rude

Little things add up to a lot in an interview. Students should know their interviewer's name *and how to pronounce it*. If they're unsure, they should ask politely—and without embarrassment—at the onset of the interview. They should shake hands firmly and be polite and courteous throughout. Finally, students mustn't forget the thank-you note!

Chapter 6:
Choosing the Right College

For families with college-bound students, the final years of high school are a very stressful time. Parents often worry that they are not doing enough and leaving their children at a disadvantage; students often feel overwhelmed by the challenge of maintaining academic and extracurricular workloads in an increasingly competitive environment. In fact, students can become so consumed with the details of *how* to get into a certain college that they forget to ask whether they really want to attend that college!

These students are doing things backwards. I believe that students should be just as selective about choosing which colleges to apply to as colleges are about choosing which students to accept. After all, given the enormous impact this decision can have on a student's future—not to mention the large financial costs involved—students and their families should be trying to make as wise and informed decisions as possible throughout the entire admissions process.

This chapter is meant to help students and their parents choose the right college. In the first two sections, I list some general considerations that should be factored into any decision about which colleges to apply to and attend. In subsequent sections, I introduce readers to some different kinds of colleges: liberal arts colleges and community colleges. Although I've focused more on large private universities and state schools so far, these aren't the only options out there. In fact, some of the *best* educational opportunities available in the U.S. are, as I'll argue, some of the lesser known.

6.1 Five Important Considerations

Stephen, a student who grew up watching his mother work as a nurse, has known his whole life that he wants to be a doctor. A hardworking student who made up for what he lacked in natural ability through hard work and diligence, he was delighted to find that he had been accepted to Johns Hopkins University: an institution particularly well-known for its medical school. Stephen and his mother felt that his future was now assured. The hard part, they thought, was over and done with. However, once at Hopkins, Stephen found himself surrounded by hundreds of students who were just as motivated as him. To make matters worse, many of these students had more native aptitude or were better trained for the rigors of the tough pre-medical curriculum. For the first time in his life, hard work just wasn't enough to help Stephen excel. In an environment that mercilessly distinguishes the best from the rest, where grading on a curve is a norm, Stephen found himself losing ground. His undergraduate grades suffered. And by the time he was applying to medical school, he was severely disadvantaged by his mediocre undergraduate transcript. Furthermore, having sacrificed plum research opportunities in his efforts to keep up his grades, Stephen found himself with an uncompetitive résumé. And he was not accepted into any top-tier medical school.

Why am I telling Stephen's story? Well, every spring, anxious high school seniors across the U.S. receive both good and bad news from the colleges they have applied to. For many of these students—and their parents—this feels like the end of a long hard journey. Everyone has worked overtime, sacrificing time and resources to make sure these students end up with the best possible college options at the end of their high school career. Students who get into their dream school feel their future is assured; students who are left only with "safeties" feel that their lives "are over." Now it is true that the choice of college is hugely significant, potentially life-changing. This is why it's so important to make sure that a student find the right-fit college. But students and their families mustn't lose sight of the fact that in the U.S., an individual's career only *begins* with the choice of college. An undergraduate institution is only a jumping-off point: pretty much every career goal still remains a real possibility for all those students who fail to get into their dream school. Everything depends on what students do once they arrive on campus. Lots of students at Harvard would, like Stephen, have been better served in their long-term goals if they *hadn't* gotten into their dream schools. Now the same isn't necessarily true in many other countries. In fact, most immigrant parents will be speaking from experience when they emphasize the importance of name brand. In many other countries—and at different times in this country—students who failed to get into the right college could be significantly disadvantaged for years to come.

Unsurprisingly, then, what most immigrant families do when college responses arrive is pick the school with the most prestigious name or the highest ranking. While this is certainly an efficient way to come to a decision, it is not always in the student's best interests. For a student such as Stephen, for example, Johns Hopkins was quite obviously the wrong fit. Attending this institution ended up hurting rather than facilitating Stephen's ability to achieve his long-term goals. Had Stephen done more research into the school before turning in his acceptance, he might have realized that the highly charged and ultra-competitive nature of the student body would not have been the best academic environment for a student with his particular learning style. In fact, if Stephen had attended a different school, he would most likely have received higher grades, stood out from among his peers, and earned acceptance into some of the very same medical schools that ultimately rejected him.

Of course, many students don't have as specific a picture of their future as Stephen did. But there are several things all students should consider in identifying right-fit colleges:

1. Degrees and majors offered
2. Location and setting
3. School size and demographics
4. Public v. private schools
5. Financial considerations

Degrees and majors offered

Some majors are not offered at every school. For example, not many schools offer a degree in journalism. And only two Ivy League schools—Cornell and the University of Pennsylvania — offer degrees in business. In fact, most liberal arts colleges won't offer options in business or engineering. Therefore students should make sure that the majors they are seriously considering are offered in the schools they apply to.

Location and setting

Does a student need the quiet of a rural environment or the bustle of an big city? Is it in a student's best interest to stay closer to home, or is it time for him or her to develop some independence?

The issue of location and setting is not just a matter of personal preference (though for lots of students, it's *mainly* that). Although almost all college will have institutional connections with the nearest major urban center—Cornell, for example, though "in the middle of nowhere," offers lots of summer opportunities in New York City—it still remains true that the NYU student, for example, will have opportunities that the Dartmouth student won't.

Studying in a major urban center allows students to undertake internships or part-time jobs *at the same time* as their studies (and not just during summers or exchange terms). This consideration is more important for some majors and some students than others.

School size and demographics

Like the issue of location, the size and demographic makeup of a school is largely a matter of personal taste. But it can have a profound impact on a student's college experience.

Students who tend to be shy and retiring or who thrive only when provided with a lot of personal attention should consider private colleges, perhaps even small liberal arts colleges. Public schools can be overwhelming for such students because of the sheer size of the student body, which necessarily results in very large classes and limited access to professors and administrative support.

Public versus private

For many students, the choice between public and private school is largely governed by financial considerations. But parents should not *assume* that private colleges are unaffordable. Many private schools, especially the more selective schools, have surprisingly generous financial aid policies and will do what it takes to attract a highly qualified student.

Also, parents should factor in the graduation rates of a particular institution when calculating expected costs. A "cheaper" school where students take an average of six years to graduate because of limited seats in core classes might end up costing as much as a private school where students generally graduate in four years. Of course, there are lots of other factors that can affect the overall cost of attending a college. Given the centrality of financial considerations for a lot of families, I'll devote the next section to this topic.

6.2 Financial Considerations

Many families don't consider financial factors early enough in the college admissions process. This is often because it is uncomfortable or painful for parents to discuss the reality of family finances with children. However, given the ever-rising cost of tuition, families really cannot wait until *after* admissions letters and financial aid offers arrive to evaluate the reality of their financial situation.

In fact, the economic climate has significantly impacted students' college application patterns: cost-conscious students are applying to public schools in record numbers. However, public schools are facing their own budgetary crises and are seeking to cap enrollment to cut cost. The current economic crisis is affecting not only individuals but also institutions. Endowments and state aid are on the decline, and both public and private schools have found it necessary to adjust their budgets and adopt provisionary measures that can sometimes dramatically impact a student's chances. So although many schools are trying to prioritize student financial aid, opting to reduce operating costs and freeze the hiring of new faculty, others are choosing to turn away students who would have been admitted in a more favorable economic climate.

The effect of all this is a squeeze on students and an increase in selectivity. The UCs, for example, received a record number of applications in 2010 but cut the actual number of acceptances offered, all while implementing a tuition hike.[69] What does all of this mean for the family that must take financial considerations into account when developing a college application strategy?

Here are three tips for navigating the financial issues around college admissions:

---

[69] Steinberg, Jacques. "University of California System Reports Rise in Applications, Not Admissions." *New York Times.* 07 Apr 2009.

1. Students must make sure to meet all application deadlines: college application deadlines *and* financial aid deadlines.

2. Students must get informed about their financial aid profile.

3. Students must manage their admissions expectations.

Meet all deadlines

Many students in California rely on the California State University (CSU) system for their "safety" schools—backup options in case admission to a UC or a private university isn't forthcoming. However, the CSU system, like the UC system, is getting squeezed on both ends: it has seen a 28% increase in applications even as it deals with budget cuts that will not accommodate a larger student body.[70]

In order to help cap enrollment, the most popular Cal State campuses (Sonoma State University and San Jose State University) are enforcing a new November 30 deadline for freshman applicants.[71] Note that the *purpose* of this deadline is to minimize the number of applications. Schools are hoping that students will fail to apply on time and thus disqualify themselves. Students who miss critical deadlines will severely limit their college options. They shouldn't expect that their applications will be considered anyway.

Whatever college a student is applying to, he or she should remember that students who miss application deadlines give colleges a great reason to reject them. And colleges really don't need any reason at all to reject a candidate—they need reasons to accept a candidate.

---

[70] Chea, Terence. "College Applications Rise, but Budgets Cap Enrollment." *USA Today*. 14 Jan 2010.

[71] California State University Admissions. "Admission, Application and Fee Information." Web. 18 Feb 2011.

Finally, a word about financial aid deadlines. Private student loan programs have been affected by the recent economic downturn. Fortunately, federal student loan programs, which offer the most generous terms, are protected by law. However, because colleges anticipate greater demand for financial aid, students must be sure to fill out the appropriate forms in a timely fashion and meet all deadlines for both state and federal loan programs.

The financial aid profile: get informed

If there is a silver lining in all this financial turmoil, it's the fact that families previously ineligible for financial aid may now qualify due to the depreciation they've experienced in home and/or investment values. Families should check their financial aid profile by using online calculators or by consulting with a financial aid specialist. The FAFSA website (http://www.fafsa.ed.gov) should be one of their first ports of call for additional information.

Manage admissions expectations

As I've stressed above, the economic crisis has made college admissions all the more competitive. Colleges are finding that they must turn away students with financial needs. Now this is generally only true of borderline students. Colleges will always make room and find financial incentives for the truly exceptional student. But for other candidates, who might very well have been accepted during flusher times, financial need is now something that may factor into the admissions decision.

If finances are a genuine constraint, students *must* apply to some schools that will view them as exceptional, either because their academic profile is significantly higher than the school's average or because their extracurricular profile holds something of interest to the school. These schools are more likely to offer financial aid and/or scholarships as incentives for extraordinary applicants.

Students should also note that *private schools may in fact end up offering a better deal than state schools*. It may be useful to seek the advice of a college counselor to pinpoint those schools that might find a particular student's profile compelling.

Also, students who are eyeing public colleges, whether state schools or community colleges, should remember that these historic "safeties" are becoming increasingly competitive. As I mentioned before, both the UC and the CSU systems are hiking tuition and cutting down on overall numbers, even as record numbers of applications are pouring in. In fact, a recent *USA Today* article reported that CSU is "seeking to reduce enrollment by an unprecedented 40,000 students over two years."[72] That's a significant number and *will* impact admissions policies. Admissions committees will have to be more selective. The days of being guaranteed a spot at one of California's public schools are over.

Although the situation may seem dire, families shouldn't despair. Look hard enough—and plan carefully enough—and students will find colleges that they can afford. There are thousands of colleges in the U.S.: many, many more than the average immigrant family is aware of. In the next two sections, I'll discuss two options that many students fail to even consider: liberal arts colleges and community colleges.

6.3 Liberal Arts Colleges

Quite possibly, most readers will have heard the term "liberal arts college" but won't have any idea what it really means. In this section, I'm going to introduce and then ultimately advocate liberal arts colleges. I think these institutions offer some of the best educational opportunities to be found *anywhere*. And yet they're an option that immigrant families in particular are not taking advantage of.

---

[72] Chea, Terence. "College Applications Rise, but Budgets Cap Enrollment." *USA Today.* 14 Jan 2010.

There are two types of private institutions: universities and colleges. A university, by definition, is an institution that is comprised of both an undergraduate *and* a graduate program. Liberal arts colleges generally do not have graduate schools.

This explains to a certain extent why the average immigrant family is not as familiar with liberal arts colleges as they are with universities. Many first-generation immigrants came to the U.S. with undergraduate degrees already in hand, with the express purpose of continuing their graduate studies in the U.S. As a result, we are all familiar with schools like MIT, UC Berkeley, and the University of Michigan. We are less familiar with Harvey Mudd College, although it has one of the best undergraduate engineering programs in the nation. This lack of information puts immigrant students at a severe disadvantage because it prevents them from exploring some of the best options the U.S. education system has to offer.

First let's look a bit more closely at what a liberal arts college is. The Annapolis Group, a non-profit alliance of the nation's top liberal arts colleges, characterizes the essence of a liberal arts education in the following way.

> A liberal arts education is a way of knowing and living, an individualized process of growth focused on intellectual engagement and involvement that is deeply personal, highly communal and grounded in the development of critical and analytical thinking, effective and persuasive communication, and active and ethical engagement.[73]

This is not the school for the student who is absolutely sure of his or her career goals and wants to get from point A to point B in the quickest way possible. For example, a student who wants to become a pharmacist sooner rather than later is best served by applying to a school with a five-year pharmacy program. However, for students who don't have such specific aims, a liberal arts education is one of the best luxuries they can

---

[73] The Annapolis Group. "About Liberal Arts Colleges." Web. 18 Feb 2011.

experience. Liberal arts colleges provide fertile, nurturing intellectual environments in which students can think, learn and stretch themselves while figuring out what to commit to.

Now it's true that students at universities can also spend a year or two finding themselves before settling on a major. So what really makes a liberal arts college unique?

Probably the most important thing for immigrant families to consider is the seemingly minor fact—already mentioned in passing—that liberal arts colleges are only for undergraduates. This makes a significant difference to a student's educational experience. Most families are not aware that in a university, the majority of funding and resources are allocated to the graduate program. Why? Because it is graduate students who bring a university prestige and endowments through their research. Undergraduates just don't take top priority. Undergraduate teaching will inevitably be passed on to graduate students, and students might spend four years at a university without becoming a recognizable face to a single professor. Compare: at a school like UC Berkeley, lecture halls hold up to six hundred students and the introductory physics lecturer might well be a 24-year-old Ph.D. candidate. At a liberal arts college, on the other hand, many classes are made up of no more than twenty-five students and all the professors are, well, actual professors, since there are no graduate students around!

My point can be brought home with some data, courtesy of the Annapolis Group. Although only 3% of American college graduates were educated at liberal arts colleges, liberal arts alumni account for:

- 23% of Pulitzer Prize winners in Drama, 19% of Pulitzer Price winners in History, and 18% of Pulitzer Prize winners in Poetry

- 20% of the scientists elected to the National Academy of Sciences

- 9% of all Fulbright scholars

- 8% of the nation's wealthiest CEOs (as ranked by *Forbes*)
- 19% of U.S. presidents.[74]

The moral? Immigrant parents and their students are strongly urged to consider liberal arts colleges. Schools like Williams College and Amherst College represent, in my opinion, some of the best higher educational institutions *worldwide*. Obviously, the liberal arts option isn't going to be right for everyone. But students and their families should know that it *is* an option and an excellent one at that.

6.4 Community Colleges

In the last section, we looked at liberal arts colleges, which can be as exclusive, selective, and well-endowed as private universities. In this section, I focus on a very different kind of college: the community college.

Here's a true story to get us started. Sue came to America during her senior year of high school. Having switched into the American system so late in the game, she was left without a lot of college options and had to enroll at her local community college, De Anza College, where she worked hard to improve her English skills and maintain good grades. At the end of two years, she was accepted into UCLA as a transfer student. Keeping up the hard work and making maximal use of the opportunities that came her way, she won the immigrant's dream ticket: entry into Harvard. Currently, she is a Ph.D. candidate in economics at Harvard University.

The possibility of such happy endings is one of the things that still make America great. Though flawed, the U.S. educational system provides more second chances than any other comparable system around the world. And the two-year

---

[74] The Annapolis Group. "About Liberal Arts Colleges." Web. 18 Feb 2011.

community college is one of the best ways the system keeps these possibilities alive.

One of the main functions of the community college is to provide a bridge from high school to university for those who are academically or financially unable to make the transition right away. In today's volatile economic climate, more and more families are finding the latter to be a reality: for some, the two-year college is the only financially viable option out there. Attending a community college is highly cost-effective: families save by paying less tuition (full-time tuition at a community college costs around $600 a year; full-time tuition at a UC costs $11,300 a year[75]) and because students living at home save on room and board.

For some students, the option of continuing to live at home can also be desirable for non-financial reasons. Not all high school graduates are ready to go off on their own. Many lack the mental and emotional readiness to function independently and need more time to mature under supervision. This is a critical factor that many parents neglect to consider. (In fact, it is for such reasons that many universities, including Princeton,[76] encourage students to take what is called a "gap year": a year off between high school and college during which burnt-out students are allowed to recharge their batteries, try on new responsibilities, and grow up a bit.)

Still others students simply won't have developed the academic credentials necessary to get accepted into a four-year university of choice. For these students, a two-year college can be a time to develop academically as well as emotionally.

So financial considerations aren't the only reasons to consider a two-year college. A student's personality, emotional maturity and academic readiness should be factored in as well.

---

[75] CaliforniaColleges.edu. "How Much Does College Cost?" Web. 18 Feb 2011.

[76] Arenson, Karen. "Princeton to Help Students Spend "Gap Year" Abroad." New York Times. 19 Feb 2008.

Now students facing the prospect of attending a community college should bear in mind that they still have lots of options available to them. In California, in particular, students who take a year or two at community college not only don't suffer any disadvantages, they enjoy some great benefits! California has one of the most generous and user-friendly transfer policies for students moving from the community college system into the Cal State or the UC system. Transfer students are given admissions priority—in 2010, a record 22,851 community college students made the move into the UC system[77]—and they can transfer up to sixty units of academic credit over. This means that two students can end up with the same degree from UCLA…but one might end up paying *thousands* of dollars less!

There are of course some disadvantages to attending a community college. For some students, staying at home for an extra two years can be a disaster, leading to a loss of purpose and direction. Some students become idle; others become depressed as most of their peers leave the area. And of course, even motivated and purposeful students miss out on some things, such as the dorm life and intense social interaction that is such a big part of the American college experience.

Furthermore, lower tuition rates inevitably buy fewer resources. Community colleges cannot afford the same caliber of institutional upkeep that four-year colleges can maintain. Libraries, laboratories, even faculty quality can unfortunately be compromised.

At the end of the day, the decision to attend a two-year college must be made in sober consideration of the various factors at play. For every Sue, there are many more students who don't make use of the opportunities that community colleges provide. And some of these students may have been better served by

---

[77] Mok, Harry. "More Students Use Community College to Launch Their UC Education." *UC Newsroom*. 11 Oct 2010.

taking out the loans necessary to get into an invigorating four-year school.

In closing, I want to urge parents to take seriously a claim I've made several times. In the U.S. higher education system, the choice of undergraduate college is only the beginning of things. What really matters is what happens once a student has arrived on campus. Everything still remains possible for the driven and capable community college student. But nothing is guaranteed, not even for the Harvard student. To drive the point home, I'm going to leave readers with another true story, a cautionary tale diametrically opposed to Sue's inspiring story.

Edward was a superstar high school student. Valedictorian, national award-winning violinist, student-body leader, Siemens Westinghouse finalist. Since elementary school, his mother had groomed him for Ivy success, making it her full-time job to seek out the best music schools, tutors, summer camps—anything and everything that would give Edward an edge. To no one's surprise, Edward was accepted into Harvard. Two years later, he dropped out. His explanation? He was so burnt-out from all the energy he had expended getting *into* Harvard that he lost all motivation once he was there. He had never had the chance to set any goals or develop any interests *other* than getting into Harvard, and when he finally got there, he wasn't sure what he was doing there.

Edward's story, unfortunately, is more common than Sue's. Parents must realize that the acceptance letter isn't a finish line but a starting line.

*   *   *

In this chapter, I discussed several issues that should be considered when trying to find the "right fit" college for a student. As we've seen, some factors are quantifiable (tuition, for example). Others are less concrete—but not thereby less important.

This is one reason why it is highly advisable for students to visit the campuses of potential colleges whenever possible. The campus visit often helps students see past the glossy promotional brochures that accompany an acceptance letter. Many students say they can sense that a college is right for them when they step on campus or slip into a classroom. At the end of the day, that elusive "feel" may be just the right thing to go with. The last section of this chapter offers students some advice for getting the most out of a campus visit.

6.5 Using the Campus Visit

When Wendell first stepped onto the Columbia campus, he was there to stay. He brought his parents, his younger sister and thirteen pieces of luggage. Like all the other matriculating freshmen, he was given an orientation package and a room key. But when he opened the door to his tiny dorm room, he was sure he had made a mistake. There was hardly room for one student, let alone two (Wendell and his roommate). Unsurprisingly, when Wendell's family left to go back home, they took much of Wendell's luggage back with him. Wendell's experience is not uncommon, especially among immigrant families for whom—as I described above—choosing a college is often a matter of consulting the latest rankings.

Families who are willing to approach the process differently, as I am urging they do, can avoid surprises like Wendell's. I strongly recommend that families invest the time and energy into making a campus visit, if not before applying, then certainly before accepting an offer. Doing so can help students avoid worse mistakes than Wendell's.

The campus visit helps families work through the confusing and abstract-seeming elements of the application process and encourages them to articulate and prioritize what they are concretely looking for in a college. In fact, for many families, the campus tour is often the first step in creating a viable college list. While there is a lot of useful information available on a school's website, nothing compares to the experience of stepping onto the actual campus, interacting with the student body and checking out the surrounding neighborhoods. Gary Ross of Colgate University puts it this way:

> Common sense would suggest—and surveys prove—that the college visit is still the most important and meaningful factor in making a college decision. Web-sites, virtual tours, and DVDs can be and are incredibly helpful in the overall college search process, but they simply do not equate to actually being on a campus, physically touring the grounds, and picturing life there for the next four years.[78]

For some, campus visits will weed out certain colleges. A school such as NYU may seem exciting in theory, but the urban environment and the lack of a traditional campus may be overwhelming in person. For others, the experience can be motivational—especially if a student falls in love with a particular school. Juniors might find their flagging energies revitalized by being able to picture their possible futures more concretely. Such enthusiasm is invaluable in surviving the college application process!

A college visit can also be a great help in answering the question, "Why this particular college?" Admissions officers are always looking for students who can demonstrate a specific, informed interest in their particular school above all others.

Here are two pieces of concrete advice for families willing to undertake the campus visit. First of all, campus visits should be scheduled during a student's junior year. Families that wait until *after* the admissions process is completed are making less-informed decisions. Plus, many colleges send out acceptance letters in April and expect a commitment by early May. This

---

[78] QuintCareers.com. "Answers to Common College Admissions Questions." Web. 18 Feb 2011.

doesn't leave much time for campus visits...even though it's senior spring!

Second of all, families should plan to visit a school *while classes are in session* in order to get an authentic experience. Although it would be convenient to visit Yale during the Christmas vacation, students will find themselves touring an empty campus. And more importantly, the admissions office will be closed! Furthermore, many schools allow prospective applicants to sit in on a class or even spend a night in the dorms; but students obviously won't be able to take advantage of these options when school is not in session.

What are some of the things students should look for when they visit a college?

1. Class sizes and student-teacher ratios can be found on any college's website. But these are *average* numbers. A potential applicant to a college should try to find an undergraduate majoring in the applicant's field of interest and ask the student what his or her actual experience has been like. How large have required classes been? How easy has it been to get to know professors or secure research positions?

2. Again, although students can find lists of school-sponsored clubs and activities online, it's only when they get on campus that they'll be able to see what's really happening and vibrant. Campus bulletin boards are a great place to gather information: students will see flyers posted from every student interest group imaginable.

3. Students should take a walk through the surrounding neighborhood. Chances are good that students won't want to spend all their time on campus. In fact, for many schools, particularly those in urban areas, the surrounding neighborhood is a crucial part of the college experience.

4. Although students can find out what their housing options are online, they should go see for themselves what the situation is. (Students who have to or want to live off-campus for a while should definitely scout out the surrounding neighborhood.)

Of course, information about housing options and student clubs doesn't amount to anything like a full picture of all a college has to offer. The campus tour is a subjective experience, and many students find that they can't exactly articulate why they've fallen in love with one school and out of love with another. These vague feelings and intuitions shouldn't be disregarded, however. At the end of the day, it is the student who is going to have to live, work, and learn at the college for the next four years. Feeling at home is going to be crucial.

A final note about campus visits and interviews: students should find out *well before they show up* whether colleges offer on-campus interviews. Most schools that do on-campus interviews schedule them for the fall semester, near the beginning of the high school student's senior year. This means that in order to take full advantage of this option, students should have a good sense of where they intend to apply *before* senior year begins. Although this will obviously take a good deal of careful advance planning, I urge students to take advantage of the on-campus interview whenever the option is made available. Many families are tempted to skip the interview, given the extra constraints these commitments place on travel plans and the extra stress it puts on a family trip. But remember that *most* of the students who get into Harvard every year have had interviews![79] They've taken every opportunity available to make a favorable impression on the university and demonstrate the seriousness of their intent.

*　　*　　*

---

[79] de Vise, Daniel. "How Important is the Admissions Interview?" *Washington Post.* 02 Aug 2010.

The right college is not always, or even usually, the biggest-name college or the highest-ranked college. In the U.S., a person's undergraduate college affiliation guarantees nothing. Nor does it rule out anything. What matters is what a student does when he or she arrives at a college. This is why it is so important for a student to prioritize finding a college where he or she can thrive. Not all students will thrive at a big, bustling Ivy. Some will...but others will get lost. Though this is a hard message for many students, especially those from immigrant families, to take to heart, I urge my readers to try.

Chapter 7:
Advice by School Year

"Preparing for college is a four-year process." So says the University of Michigan, one of the most popular and well-respected public institutions in the U.S.[80] Now the average freshman (or even sophomore) is busy enough adjusting to high school. Planning for something that seems so far away might seem unnecessary. However, every decision that a high school student makes impacts his or her chances of college success. Now I'm certainly not advocating that freshmen and sophomores make all—or in fact any—of their choices by considering what college officers might like. But I think that all high school students and their parents should know what the potential consequences of their choices are so they can make informed decisions. In this chapter, I bring together the advice offered throughout the first six chapter of this book, re-organizing tips by high school year. I'll address freshmen and sophomores first, and then juniors and seniors.

---

[80] University of Michigan Office of Undergraduate Admissions. "Preparing for College." Web. 18 Feb 2011.

7.1 Words of Advice for Freshmen and Sophomores

The first two years of high school used to be a breeze. Students could still make mistakes, fall behind on their studies, make some thoughtless decisions…. They still had time to get their act together, because back then, things only really started to matter junior year. Times have changed. Nowadays, students are starting to prepare for college at an earlier and earlier age.

In this section, I'll discuss the underclassman calendar and explain what the freshman's and sophomore's priorities should be. These first two years of high school don't demand the same level of commitment as the last two years; however, they must be taken seriously…especially sophomore year. And the top priority *for all four years* remains the same: GPA.

GPA

The most important thing for both freshmen and sophomores to focus on is schoolwork. The higher the GPA and the stronger the strength of the curriculum, the better.

Most schools look at a student's entire four-year high school transcript when evaluating the student's academic profile. The University of California is unique in that it uses sophomore- and junior-year grades to determine *eligibility*, and then considers the whole high school transcript for *admissions*. But the vast majority of schools, whether private or public, look at four years of coursework.

Now most schools don't have a minimum cut-off GPA. However, as I've repeatedly emphasized, the high school transcript remains the single most significant factor for gaining admission into college, whether private or public. The University of Virginia sets out its advice with crystal clarity, telling sophomores to "Take a strong academic program. Take tough courses in English, math, foreign language, science, and social science.

Make your schedule tougher each year."[81] So does the University of Michigan: "You should take 4 or 5 academic courses each term, and try to take as many accelerated, honors, or advanced classes that are available in subjects that you excel in."[82]

Students should really take note of what these admissions offices are saying. Remember, GPA is not just a number! Let's analyze all the various components that these schools referred to. Schools will look at:

1. the subjects taken (an A in Studio Art doesn't count for as much as an A in English).

2. the difficulty level of classes (an A in general Biology isn't nearly as valuable as an A in AP Biology).

3. the number of years students have taken classes in core academic subjects. Though different schools have different prerequisites, most will require *at least* two years in each of the core academic subjects and four in some. (The UCs, for example, require only two years of history classes but a full four years of English.[83])

4. the number of classes taken in any given semester. In normal circumstances, students shouldn't take fewer than five courses during the school year, and they shouldn't think to use summers to make up for classes not taken during the school year. Summer school should only be used to *supplement* academic year schoolwork, not to make up or replace academic year schoolwork.

Course selection is particularly important sophomore year because it impacts student eligibility for advanced classes in

---

[81] University of Virginia Office of Undergraduate Admission. "Admission and Application Tips." Web. 18 Feb 2011.

[82] University of Michigan Office of Undergraduate Admissions. "Preparing for College." Web. 18 Feb 2011.

[83] University of California Admissions. "The Subject Requirement." Web. 18 Feb 2011.

following years, and obviously, taking advanced classes is crucial to a student's college admissions prospects. For example, students who opt *not* to take an honors science sophomore year may not be allowed to enroll in an AP science junior year. Similarly, dropping out of the honors track in math during sophomore year might prevent a student from being able to take AP Calculus BC as a senior.

Of course, students shouldn't just aim for the maximally difficult course load. When it comes to course selection, it is important to be realistic about a student's abilities. As a rule of thumb, students who receive a C (or worse) should strongly consider dropping down a level of difficulty in that subject or otherwise rearranging their course load so as to make things more manageable. Cs *will* compromise the student's eligibility at the most competitive schools, such as the Ivy League schools (though to be frank, the student who struggles academically in high school doesn't have a realistic shot at these schools anyway). Being over-ambitious about course selection can harm a student's chances of getting into other excellent but less-selective colleges. So students should aim for the most rigorous course load consistent with maintaining at least Bs.

Standardized tests

Standardized tests—SAT or ACT scores—is the number two factor affecting admissions decisions. This is something for sophomores to start thinking about. With a little bit of planning, sophomores can significantly manage the stress of standardized test taking and invest in their future sanity.

First of all, sophomores who have the option should take both the PSAT (given in October) and the PLAN (a pre-ACT test). Students' scores in these tests will give a sense of their level of readiness. Students who receive low scores should consider starting test prep *as sophomores.* Students who excel at standardized testing and who receive very high scores can consider taking the SAT or ACT sophomore year. Now there are both upsides and downsides to this decision, so it shouldn't be made without consulting a counselor. On the upside, the student who aces the SAT or ACT as a sophomore will have freed up his or her junior year; this spare time can be translated into exceptional extracurricular activities. Alternatively, the student who does well on the SAT or ACT as a sophomore but then *aces* it on a second try junior year may look more attractive—faster and more "on top of things"—than the student who does exactly the same thing and gets exactly the same scores, but does it all one year later. However, most sophomores are not ready, emotionally or academically, to put their best foot forward on a big standardized test. Most sophomores will end up having to retake the test a third time, which would look worse than getting started later and taking the test just twice.

Sophomores should also start planning out their SAT Subject Test schedules. Many students should consider taking their first test in May or June of sophomore year, picking the subject they most excelled at to cut their teeth on. Students should also know that for some of the SAT Subject Tests, there's really only one good opportunity to sit the test. For example, for most students there's only one year in which it makes sense for them to take the SAT Subject Test in World History: the year students take World History in school. Most students won't ever cover that material again in high school. For subjects like World History, students must be doubly sure to prepare very carefully the *first* time around. If a student isn't happy with his or her June World History SAT score, that student won't be able to retake the test until October, at which point the student will have to review World History while also juggling U.S. History in school!

Finally, students should know that they don't have to wait until they're taking AP-level coursework to sit the SAT Subject Tests. These tests do not pre-suppose AP-level knowledge.

Despite all of these academic obligations, freshmen and sophomores cannot neglect their extracurricular activities. Freshman year is a great time to explore potential passions, but sophomores must start focusing and refining their activities, figuring out where their priorities and interests really lie.

In conclusion, I want to urge parents of freshmen and especially sophomores to take this opportunity to sit down with their children and identify deadlines, articulate goals, weigh options and map out a plan of attack as a family. It is not too early. High school students must hit the ground running...and obviously, the time to figure out *where* to head is *before* take-off!

College admissions today are so competitive that the successful student is the one that starts early and plans ahead. To illustrate this, I'll spend the next three sections introducing three very different students and showing how the decisions they made as sophomores impacted their college prospects.

7.2 Sophomore-Year Case Study: Frank, the Underachiever

When Frank first came to me, he was the classic under-achieving sophomore. A "nice" kid by all accounts, he just wasn't particularly interested in anything academic. And although this had been true throughout his entire student career, it became a more pressing issue as he progressed through high school with no discernible increase in interest or motivation.

As readers can see, Frank's freshman-year grades got him off on the wrong foot:

Course	Fall Semester	Spring Semester
Geometry	A	B
Biology	B	C
English	B	B
Spanish	B	B
History	B	A
PE	A	A
Academic GPA	3.1	

Notice that Frank's first-term GPA was higher than his second-term GPA. This phenomenon isn't that surprising: later coursework builds on earlier coursework and so assumes mastery and at least partial retention of earlier material. But on top of that, some students have trouble sustaining an effort, so their grades flag as the year goes on.

Now when Frank came to me, he brought the following first-quarter progress report (mid-term report after ten weeks of school):

Course	First Quarter
Algebra 2/ Trigonometry	A
Chemistry	B
English	B
Spanish 2	B
History	A
PE	A
Academic GPA	**3.4**

Although Frank did better than the previous term, remember that Frank's grades tended to go *down* as he got further and further into the school year. If past trends continued, Frank's GPA would only go down from this 3.4.

Frank and his family needed me to realistically assess Frank's strengths and weaknesses and help him understand his college prospects. I encouraged Frank to think about whether he wanted to target the more selective public schools (the UCs) and the mid-level private schools or whether he'd be happy to focus on the lower-tier schools (public or two-year). Articulating a goal would be a necessary first step to figuring out what would have to be done to realize the goal.

Now although Frank came to me quite early in his high school career, and so still had time to strategically position himself and make a material difference to his chances, some possibilities were already closed off for him. This is how Frank's situation looked from the perspective of different categories of schools.

Top-tier private and public schools
(Stanford, the Ivy League schools, Berkeley/UCLA)

Even though he was just a sophomore, Frank had pretty much given up any realistic shot of getting admitted to schools of this level. Knowing this was important: Frank could focus his energies on maximizing his chances at schools where he stood a real chance of getting admitted.

Mid-tier private schools
(Pepperdine, Boston University, Pitzer College)

The best thing Frank could do to raise his chances of getting into one of these schools was to dramatically improve his academics: raise his GPA, especially in the five core academic areas, and post a strong SAT score. But Frank also needed to balance his academics with some extracurricular activities.

I encouraged Frank and his family to have a frank discussion about whether Frank would have the motivation and energy to both raise his academic performance *and* cultivate extracurricular activities. This would require Frank to be a *lot* more active, energetic and motivated than he had ever been before, even if he limited his extracurricular projects to the summer.

Mid-tier public schools
(Irvine, Davis, Santa Barbara)

In order to be even *eligible* for any of the UCs, a student has to maintain a GPA of *at least* 3.0 in 10th and 11th grade. But realistically, given the competitive nature of UC admissions, Frank's GPA needed to be considerably higher.

Now Frank and his family needed to understand what would be necessary to target these mid-tier public schools. They also needed to know whether everyone involved was willing to make the necessary sacrifices to give Frank a realistic shot. Because although it was possible for Frank to make himself a contender at these schools, *a lot* of hard work would be required from *everyone* involved.

First, Frank needed to dramatically raise his level of academic achievement. This meant he needed to find greater motivation as well as better time management skills, since he *also* needed to start preparing for the SATs. In order to make all of this possible, I strongly recommended that Frank drop *everything* else he had going on and focus solely on academics. In particular, Frank needed to give up the time-consuming leisure activities that prevented him from achieving his academic goals. This required a firm helping hand from Frank's parents, who were advised to curtail Frank's free access to the Internet.

Readers must remember that the UCs are very different from private colleges. Simple numbers and academics matter a lot more; extracurricular activities matter a lot less. So my recommendations were designed specifically for the *UCs* and specifically for *Frank.*

Lower-tier private and public schools
(UC Merced, Cal States, University of San Francisco)

Frank had another option, though, one that would allow him to have a more balanced high school life. Frank was still a realistic candidate at the lower-tier schools, and he didn't have to do much to keep things that way. He would need to work hard enough to avoid any more Cs; he would need to make sure he met the basic academic requirements for each college. But he wouldn't need to raise the difficulty of his coursework. He'd also still have the time to pursue the hobbies he enjoyed without worrying about how colleges would perceive such activities.

*　　*　　*

As we can see from the case study of Frank, sophomores have already marked out a starting position on the college selection process. The top-tier schools were no longer a realistic option for Frank. But a lot of other great schools, including mid-tier private and public schools, were within striking range. Deciding which category of school to target was really urgent for Frank. He needed to decide what really mattered to him, and then take action with full knowledge of the likely consequences of his choice.

As it turned out, Frank was strongly motivated to turn things around. After meeting with me as a sophomore, Frank decided to take things to the next level. He loaded up on AP courses as a junior and a senior and continually raised his GPA from semester to semester, ending up with almost straight-As, some great AP scores, and an SAT score of over 2200. Frank's change of heart also won over several of his teachers, who wrote great recommendations on his behalf. Finally, Frank extended this hard work to packaging his application, writing compelling essays that convinced admissions officers at several top-25 private colleges to take a chance on him despite his weak start.

7.3 Sophomore-Year Case Study: Annie, the Student at a Crossroads

Annie was a sophomore with an average academic profile. Her grades weren't bad, but they were far from perfect. When Annie came to me early in her sophomore year, she was at a true crossroads. She hadn't done anything to permanently harm her admissions chances, but any future misstep could close off some possibilities and have a detrimental effect on her college application profile. Let's look at Annie's freshman-year grades:

Course	Fall Semester	Spring Semester
Algebra 2/ Trigonometry	A	A
Biology	A	A
English	A	B
Spanish	B	B
History	B	B
PE	A	A
Academic GPA	**3.5**	

And here are her sophomore-year first-quarter grades:

Course	Fall Semester
Honors Precalculus	A
Honors Chemistry	A
English	A
Spanish 2	B
AP World History	B
PE	A
Academic GPA	**3.8**

Annie and her family had to make a sober assessment of Annie's prospects. Her grades so far were average to above-average. And these were the grades she received during the easiest phase of her high school career—schoolwork was only going to get more difficult. Moreover, Annie obviously had strengths in math and science, but struggled with the humanities.

So Annie and her family had to make some hard decisions about her future. Specifically, they needed to decide whether Annie would push really hard to target a top-tier private school or whether she would be allowed the freedom to pursue whatever activities and classes interested her. Taking the latter path would allow her to have a more balanced high school experience, but it would likely cost her the chance of getting into an upper-tier private school. As we did with Frank, let's see what Annie's chances were at different categories of schools.

Top-tier private schools
(Cornell, Johns Hopkins, Northwestern)

Many families with students like Annie cling to the hope that their child will get into an upper-tier private like the ones listed above. This isn't impossible. But families should be very realistic in estimating the effort and commitment required to make the cut. To be competitive at upper-tier schools, students must maintain a near-perfect academic profile while building a strong extracurricular profile.

In Annie's case, her sophomore-year class selection was suitably aggressive, but she needed to improve her grades. She also had to make sure she signed up for a highly rigorous junior-year course load with a good number of APs...and she couldn't let her GPA slip as the coursework grew more demanding. Annie also needed to start positioning herself to achieve Ivy-level scores on her SATs (or ACT) her junior year.

Non-academic factors are also extremely important for getting into schools of this caliber. In Annie's case, they were especially important, because they would need to compensate for the early weakness in Annie's transcript. Annie needed to build a focused and convincing extracurricular profile, one that would differentiate her from other students and demonstrate her leadership ability.

Public schools (UCLA, UC Berkeley, UC Irvine)

Remember that admissions at the public schools is much more heavily driven by academics, especially at the upper-tier public schools. For example, both UC Berkeley and the University of Illinois Urbana-Champaign are prestigious public schools that receive so many applicants that they practice very formulaic, numbers-driven admissions. Though extracurricular activities can enhance a student's chance of gaining admission, they will not have the same impact that they do in private school admissions. (This is why some students who are rejected by UC Berkeley can get into a school like Cornell.)

For Annie to aim for the upper-tier public schools, she needed to maximize her GPA and get cracking on the SATs, even as a sophomore. Annie also needed to strongly prioritize her academics over other things: she could probably handle some extracurricular activities, but she needed to put such commitments decisively in second place.

This is not an easy choice for a sophomore to make. It requires adopting and sticking to a narrowly focused admissions strategy. But for families with compelling reasons, usually financial, for targeting the upper-tier publics, this is the best route.

Second-tier private schools (Boston College, NYU, USC)

There were two strategies Annie could use to target these schools.

To get into schools of this caliber, a student's grades don't need to be perfect, although they must still demonstrate an ability to succeed in college level work. So one strategy available for Annie was to maintain her current level of academic achievement while developing her extracurricular profile to a comparable level. Concretely, this meant that Annie had to maintain a similar GPA while signing up for a somewhat more rigorous schedule her junior year. She didn't, however, need to max out on APs. For example, she could've consolidated in her areas of natural strength and taken advanced courses in math and science, sticking to the regular track in the humanities. She also didn't need to maintain a 4.0 to target these schools, although if her GPA *fell* from her sophomore level of achievement, she'd have to start looking at private schools the next tier down on the tables: schools like Santa Clara University and Boston University.

The other strategy Annie could have used to target these schools could have done "double-duty" for the UCs. If Annie raised her grades to straight As and attained Ivy-level SAT or ACT scores, she would have been very competitive at these schools, even with a weaker extracurricular profile.

*   *   *

As Annie's case shows, some sophomores and their families have very hard decisions to make about where their priorities lie and which admissions strategy to adopt. Families who foresee that the UCs will be their best bet may have to encourage their children to focus very narrowly on their academics. It is very important that families are able to engage in these discussions in a productive and honest way.

Another thing to take away from Annie's case is the following. I agreed with Annie and her parents that Annie *could* improve her grades, that she was a bright but comparatively lazy student whose 3.5 freshman year wasn't representative of her abilities. But of course, this isn't always going to be the case. Some students work very hard for their 3.5. Parents of such students should be realistic about how much more their children can achieve academically. They might want to help their children foster other strengths, whether these turn out to be great leadership skills or unusual athletic talents.

All things considered, I advised Annie to focus on her areas of natural aptitude—math and science—and to develop a coherent application profile around these strengths. However, Annie decided to take on extra challenges all around and loaded up on AP humanities courses as well. This, of course, demonstrated a willingness to seek out academic challenges—a trait looked upon favorably by colleges. However, Annie didn't manage to ace these humanities courses. She ended every term with a mix of Bs and As.

Ultimately, Annie was not able to develop the well-rounded, high-level academic profile necessary to crack the top-ten most selective colleges. She did, however, receive several great offers from top-twenty schools with particularly strong math and science programs.

7.4 Sophomore-Year Case Study: Derek, the Model Student

Derek maintained a perfect academic record despite taking a very challenging course load sophomore year. Let's take a look at his freshman-year grades.

Course	Fall Semester	Spring Semester
English	A	A
History	A	A
Algebra 2/ Trigonometry	A	A
Biology	A	A
Spanish	A	A
PE	A	A
Weighted GPA	4.0	

And here are the sophomore-year first-quarter grades he brought when he first came to see me:

Course	Fall Semester
English	A
AP World History	A
Honors Precalculus	A
Chemistry	A
Spanish 2	A
PE	A
Weighted GPA	4.2

Derek had also already taken his SATs October of sophomore year and received a score of 2320. In short, Derek was that kid that every parent holds up as the "model" student and assumes is headed straight for a top-tier college. But was he really on the right path?

Clearly, Derek's academic achievement left nothing to be desired. How could it really be improved? However, it was important for Derek not to let up, to continue pursuing the most challenging curriculum possible while maintaining as close to a perfect GPA as possible. Having scored an impressive 2320 on his SAT, he needed to find a similar level of excellence on his other standardized tests (SAT Subject Tests and APs). However, was this all Derek needed to do?

Remember that academic achievements, no matter how impressive, are never enough to get any student into one of the most selective colleges. Academic requirements are only minimum hurdles that have to be passed for an application to receive serious consideration. With that in mind, let's see what Derek's extracurricular record looked like as a sophomore:

Highlights of Derek's
Extracurricular Activities

Piano: Numerous local awards

Community service: Red Cross Club; Church activities (Thanksgiving food drive, Toys for Tots, etc.)

Mock Trial Team: Participant

Model United Nations: Participant

Let's consider how Derek's extracurricular profile would look at different kinds of schools.

Most selective schools
(Harvard, Stanford, Yale, Princeton)

Although Derek had been actively participating in many different clubs, he didn't have anything really impressive to make him a stand-out candidate. Of course, Derek's academics were impressive, but it was matched by thousands and thousands of other students. If Derek didn't have anything in his extracurricular profile to help him stand out, then he didn't have anything to help him stand out at all. In fact, it was clear that if Derek just carried on, he'd end up lacking the "wow" factor.

More specifically, there was no "story" being developed in Derek's extracurricular activities. He looked like a diligent and dutiful student, rather than a student with passions and genuine interests. An admissions officer looking at Derek's résumé would have a hard time remembering who Derek is after closing the file. This was a glaring weakness. Derek needed to sharpen the focus of his extracurricular activities and develop a more compelling résumé.

Derek also needed to consider something else. For a student to be competitive at the highest level, he needs to differentiate himself from all other applicants, *especially* those that come from his own school and his own geographical area. A school such as Stanford will never take a large number of students from one high school, no matter how qualified the group. One way for a student to stand out from his closest competitors is to position himself aggressively with regard to the *strengths* of his local high school. For example, Troy High School in southern California has a Science Olympiad team ranked fifth nationally. Harvard typically accepts two students from members of this team. Leland High School in northern California has a well-known Robotics Club. MIT typically accepts two students from this club. Palo Alto High School, also in northern California, has a newspaper that has won numerous awards from such high-profile sources as *Time* magazine. Being editor of *The Campanile* is a much more substantial achievement than being editor of any number of other high school newspapers. As a student at a high school with a very active Model U.N. team— one that yearly sent a couple of members to international Model U.N. conferences—Derek's participation, though consistent enough, looked passive and indifferent.

Other top-tier schools
(University of Chicago, Northwestern, Johns Hopkins)

These schools, while difficult to get into, are not *as* competitive as the handful discussed above. Derek just needed to keep things up in order to stand a reasonable chance of getting into a good number of them. More precisely: although Derek's extracurricular profile was only averagely strong, this was compensated for by his unimpeachable academics, which put him *above* the average accepted range at the schools listed above.

Second-tier schools (USC, NYU, Emory, Boston College)

One of the biggest factors that prohibit students from going to private colleges is cost. If a student like Derek is experiencing financial difficulty, it may be worthwhile for him to target schools like the above. An academic record like Derek's will be substantially higher than average at these schools, and will make him a prime candidate for scholarships and other honors programs at these colleges.

*　　*　　*

As it turned out, Derek was able to maintain his academic focus. He took a well-balanced and aggressive course-load junior year and senior year and continued to maintain a 4.0 average. He also performed consistently well on his SAT Subject Tests (800s in math 2 and Chemistry and 780 in English Literature) and his AP exams (5s in five different subjects his sophomore and junior years).

However, he was unable to find an extracurricular activity that really exercised his leadership and initiative. Derek was chosen to lead the Mock Trial program and he continued to participate in Model UN; he also continued to devote a decent number of hours to community service, especially through his musical activities and his church groups. However, his extracurricular résumé remained too incoherent—it was never clear, for example, why he decided to participate in the clubs he chose. And because he went to an extremely competitive public high school, his profile remained indiscernible, if not inferior, to his close competition. Ultimately Derek gained admission at several Ivy League universities, including Brown and Cornell, but failed to gain entrance to Harvard, Yale and Stanford.

*　　*　　*

The last three sections profiled three very different students. As sophomores, these students, despite all the differences in their strengths, personalities, and goals, had several options that remained within reach. However, they all had some hard decisions to make.

Bob Wise, president of the Alliance for Excellent Education, aptly describes sophomore year as the "final sorting-out year."[84] What students do as sophomores *will* make a difference: it can close off certain possibilities or bring others within striking range. This will happen regardless of whether students are aware of the consequences of their choices or not. The best thing students can do is get informed and take control of their futures. I repeat: sophomore year is not too early to be thinking about these things.

7.5 Words of Advice for Juniors

Families that first come to me after the first semester of junior year inevitably end up saying the same thing. "I wish I met you sooner." That's because there's critical information that students need at the *beginning* of junior year. And even the *averagely* busy junior has so packed and stressful a schedule that those who haven't actively managed their obligations will end up putting out fire after fire...and never getting properly on top of things.

The British philanthropist Charles Buxton once said, "You will never *find* time for anything. If you want time, you must *make* it."[85] Juniors need to make a *lot* of time. They need to make time to (a) maintain if not improve their GPA, all while (b) taking the hardest courses they've ever tried (many will be looking at AP-level material for the first time). Juniors also need to ace a whole bunch of standardized tests, including (c) the SAT or ACT; (d) one or two SAT Subject Tests; and (e) a handful of APs. And of course, (f) juniors must continue developing their extracurricular profiles. The workload can be daunting.

---

[84] Strauss, Valerie. "Sophomore Year: Between Lark and a Hard Place." *Washington Post*. 07 Feb 2006.

[85] Buxton, Charles. *Notes of Thought*. London: John Murray, 1873. §488.

This section addresses juniors and their parents and tells them how to approach junior year strategically. I advise rising juniors to create a calendar for the entire academic year, from August through June. They should then do the following:

1. Students should first fill in the dates of their finals because, as I've been emphasizing all along, GPA is the number one factor determining college admissions. Final dates are also fixed, so there's no decision to be made about when to take the tests.

2. Students should then schedule in the test date for any AP class that they are taking. (Note: the AP tests are only offered once a year, in May.)

3. Thirdly, students should enter all other fixed commitments: dates that can't be negotiated or postponed. They should also think about their extracurricular activities and when these will turn out to be the heaviest. For example, a basketball player might not know his exact practice and game schedule, but he'll know that basketball is a winter sport that will take up a lot of time from November through February.

4. Now students can strategically think about when to schedule in the SAT (or ACT) and the SAT Subject Tests. The SAT Subject tests are generally more straightforward. In most cases, students should take them in May or June of the year they complete that particular subject in school. After all, it's hardly ideal to take the SAT U.S. History test in January when the school curriculum has only covered up to the mid-1800s! However, juniors who receive a low score on an SAT Subject Test sophomore year and want to retake the test must put some thought into when to schedule the retake. For subjects that are cumulative—a foreign language or math—students can expect to improve with time. But if, say, a sophomore bombs the World History SAT and really wants to retake it because her first-choice school

doesn't accept score choice, then she will have to schedule things carefully. She will probably want to schedule the retake for early junior year, leaving time over the summer to prepare systematically.

5. What about the SAT (or ACT) itself? When students should first take the big test depends on how ready the student is. Remember, students should aim to take the SAT (or ACT) *no more than twice*, but ideally just once. This means that students who aren't approaching their goal score by, say, December of junior year should consider postponing the test until March or even May/June. However, students shouldn't leave the test until senior year.

Let's take a look at a sample junior-year schedule. Peter is a varsity basketball player signed up for several AP courses. He hasn't taken any SATs yet, so he'll need to find time for these important tests this year.

1. Peter's school finals will take place during January and June.

2. He will have to take AP tests in May.

3. His basketball commitments will keep him really busy from early November through early February.

4. Peter will be taking two SAT Subject Tests in May and June.

5. The SATs are offered every year in January, March, May, June, October, November and December. Peter is ruling out November and December because of his basketball schedule and January because of his fall semester finals. He's saving May and June for the Subject Tests...and besides, he's got AP tests and more school finals to think about. So Peter's first chance of taking the test will be October of junior year, and this will leave him time to retake the test in March, if necessary. But if Peter isn't anywhere near his target score in September, he'll have

to consider postponing his first attempt until March. If absolutely necessary, he can take both SAT Subject Tests in May and retake the SAT in June.

This schedule is obviously tailored to Peter's needs. Students who are busily involved in marching band early in the academic year, or students who have finals in December and May, will need to adjust things. Here are some further things for juniors to bear in mind as they draw up their own schedules.

GPA

Students are reminded yet again that GPA is the single most important factor in college admissions. Junior year is going to plunge students into the most academically demanding environment they've ever experienced. This means that students don't want to over-extend themselves by committing to too many extracurricular activities!

The SATs

Students are also *strongly* advised to do whatever they can to avoid having to spend the summer before senior year preparing for the SAT or ACT! Those who have done something meaningful the last summer before applications are due will look a lot more compelling to admissions officers. Plus, as I mentioned above, private schools don't look too favorably on students who wait until the last minute to take the SAT (or ACT).

Students should also remember that colleges, especially private colleges, don't respond well to students who've taken their tests in a haphazard and thoughtless fashion. For example, students who take the SAT too frequently give the impression that they are wasting a disproportionate amount of time and energy on ineffectual test prep. Admissions officers do *not* want such students in their student body! Therefore, as I emphasized above, it's wise to wait until ready.

But of course, it takes months, if not years, to be "ready" for a test like the SAT or ACT. As many students have probably already experienced, students need a certain amount of time to see meaningful improvements in their scores (minimally, eight to twelve weeks). This means, of course, that students should start their test prep *well* in advance of their proposed test date. It also means that students shouldn't plan to take the SAT on consecutive test dates: October and November, for example. There won't be enough time to make significant score gains. (Remember that colleges don't think fifty-point bumps are meaningful.)

The moral of this section is simple. Students should schedule their standardized tests carefully. They don't want to be intensively preparing for the SAT when they've got five school finals to study for. But they also want their final prep to do double duty for SAT Subject Test prep. Planning ahead will help give students the time and headspace to keep up their GPA while also getting everything else done.

*   *   *

For those readers who still have some or all of their junior year in front of them, I advise them to sit down *right now* and strategically plan the remainder of their year. All these tests and deadlines are coming, whether students are ready or not. They'll obviously go a lot better if the student is ready!

7.6 Words of Advice for Seniors

For readers who have just survived junior year, I'm afraid I have some bad news. Things are going to get worse before they get better. Once senior year hits, students will be saddled with a workload *greater* than that of junior year. As in junior year, seniors must keep up their GPA and their extracurricular activities. Any senior who hasn't finished his standardized testing has only a few more test dates to get the job done. But on top of all this, seniors have to start preparing college applications, most of which are due between the beginning of November and the end of December. The volume of work that goes into these applications is considerable—much greater than students anticipate.

I don't have any new advice to offer students at the beginning of senior year. These students must continue to apply the time-management strategies of junior year. Planning carefully is going to be crucial to surviving these last few months of mania.

I do, however, have something new and important to say to seniors who have submitted their applications *and to seniors who have already received their admissions letters.* There is a very dangerous myth circulating that senior year doesn't matter. Well, here are several stories—all 100% true—that seniors should take to heart.

- After one student was admitted to Harvard University, information surfaced showing that she had plagiarized on articles she wrote for her local newspaper, copying extensively from material found on the Internet. Most students wouldn't think this was a big deal. Harvard did. It rescinded this student's acceptance.[86]

- Several students who were admitted to the University of Washington began to cut back on their academics, dropping the more challenging courses in their schedule and allowing their grades to fall. The university rescinded *23* offers of admission.[87]

- Tom was admitted to UC Davis. During the second semester of his senior year, he received a D in English— a UC-mandated course. He also dropped his foreign language course and ended up with a 2.0 GPA. UC Davis rescinded his acceptance.[88]

---

[86] Green, Elizabeth and Russell, J. Hale. "Harvard Takes Back Hornstine Admission Offer." *Harvard Crimson.* 11 Jul 2003.

[87] Perry, Nick. "UW Revokes Admission Offers in Severe Cases of 'Senior-itis.'" *Seattle Times.* 03 Oct 2006.

[88] Franck, Marion. "A Lost Opportunity." *UC Davis Magazine.* Fall 2004.

- Kyle was admitted to the University of North Carolina (UNC). A student bright enough to earn a perfect score on his SAT, he managed to earn a 1.3 GPA during his senior year. UNC rescinded his acceptance.[89]

What all these unfortunate seniors didn't know is that all admissions decisions are *conditional* and can be revoked for a variety of reasons. The most common reason for rescinding admissions is academic. The summer after senior year, all students must send in a copy of their final transcripts. Any red flags (a particularly low GPA, failure to pass required courses, dropping more challenging classes) are dealt with according to university policy.

However, it's not just poor academic performance that can lead to the withdrawal of an offer. Harvard warns students explicitly that "admission will be revoked if you engage in behavior that brings into question your honesty, maturity, or moral character."[90] This is essentially what happened to Alice: she was found guilty of academic theft. Similarly, students can also lose their places for committing fraud on their applications. Students are warned: schools can not only rescind offers of admissions; they can also seize completed degrees should falsehoods be discovered.

Now in the past, the practice of rescinding acceptances was considered more of a private school phenomenon. But public schools are taking up this issue with a vengeance, especially the UCs. UC policy is clear: "Admission is contingent on remaining in all UC preparatory courses, maintaining a C or better in all senior-year classes listed on the application and graduating from high school."[91] There isn't much room for misinterpretation here.

In fact, all schools seem to be exercising this option with more frequency and aggressiveness. There's an explanation for this.

---

[89] Swygert, Kimberly. "Failing in His Tar Heel Bid." *Number 2 Pencil*. 26 Aug 2003. Web. 18 Feb 2011.

[90] Green, Elizabeth and Russell, J. Hale. "Harvard Takes Back Hornstine Admission Offer." *Harvard Crimson*. 11 Jul 2003.

[91] Franck, Marion. "A Lost Opportunity." *UC Davis Magazine*. Fall 2004.

Barmak Nassirian, the Associate Executive Director of the American Association of Collegiate Registrars and Admissions Officers, says, "The increasing competition at elite schools is making some institutions less tolerant of senioritis and more willing to eject a student who had already sent in an enrollment deposit.... Schools are becoming more stern about that than they were in the past."[92] The same rationale explains the UC policy. Susan Wilbur, Director of Undergraduate Admissions for the University of California, notes that "With so many strong applicants previously rejected at competitive campuses, it is absolutely incumbent upon us to uphold the integrity of the process and maintain the high standards."[93]

Having an offer rescinded is obviously devastating in and of itself. But what makes this practice particularly problematic is the timing. Senior-year grades are reported the summer *after* senior year, which means that colleges will be rescinding admissions in late July, even August. At that point, students will already have made their deposit to the school of their choice and turned down all the other schools to which they have been accepted. In reality, a student who gets his or her admissions revoked at this point will be left with no good options.

The moral of the lesson should be clear. It's not from a lack of sympathy that I strongly urge seniors to finish strong and put in a valiant effort until graduation. I think there's a good reason for the nationwide fatigue, malaise, and under-motivation that afflicts so many seniors around the nation that it has its own name: senioritis. But seniors need to know that an admissions letter is only a conditional acceptance. Students must live up to their end of the bargain by continuing to demonstrate the qualities that earned them admission in the first place.

---

[92] Gordon, Larry. "No Slack for Student Slackers." *Los Angeles Times*. 22 Jun 2007.
[93] *Ibid.*

Chapter 8: Case Studies

It is my hope that the information presented so far in this book has been useful to students navigating the college application process. While I've sprinkled examples and case studies throughout the book, I think it'll be instructive to look at a few more to help us wrap up our discussion.

Readers are invited to look through these case studies and see whether they identify with any of these students. Maybe some readers will find the motivation they need to take things to the next level. Maybe other readers will be able to get rid of some stress, knowing they're doing what they should be. Hopefully all readers will end up with a better sense of what to do to get where they want to go.

8.1 George and Emory University

George was a bright but undermotivated student at a reputable Bay Area High School. As his application profile, presented in the next two pages, shows, he worked just enough to maintain decent scores. Because of his natural aptitude, he did very well on his standardized tests without too much trouble.

Transcript

FRESHMAN YEAR		
Course	Fall Semester	Spring Semester
English	B	B
History	A-	A-
Algebra 1/ Geometry	A-	A-
Biology	B+	A-
Japanese	B+	A-
Web Design/ Photography	A	A

SOPHOMORE YEAR		
Course	Fall Semester	Spring Semester
English	A-	A-
World History	A-	A-
Algebra 2/ Trigonometry	A-	A-
Honors Chemistry	B-	B-
Japanese	A+	A-
Journalism/Art	B-	B+

JUNIOR YEAR		
Course	Fall Semester	Spring Semester
Honors English	A	A
AP U.S. History	B-	B
Precalculus	A	A
AP Biology	B	A
Japanese	B+	B+
Physics	A	A

Standardized Test Record:

SAT: 2150

Math: 710
Critical Reading: 700
Writing: 740

Math 2: 800

World History: 620

Biology: 710

U.S. History: 690

Extracurricular Activities:

COSMOS Game Design:
Four-week residential program
(summer of junior year)

Volunteer Work:
School for young Chinese students
(sophomore year)

Soccer:
Member of high school team
(freshman through junior year)

Recommendations:

Math Instructor
(junior year)

Physics Instructor
(junior year)

Intended Major:

Business

The glaring weakness in George's application, however, was his lack of extracurricular activities. He did the bare minimum in community service and sports but, like many teenagers, spent most of his free time idling on the Internet. George came to me only as a senior. It was too late for him to do anything to dramatically alter his application profile.

When it comes to a student like George, my job is to make sure he is left with as many good options as possible at the end of the process. I needed George to understand how his application would look to admissions officers at very different schools: top-tier private colleges; second-tier private colleges; and the UCs. As we'll see, George's data will look very different to different admissions officers.

Most selective (University of Pennsylvania)

Simply put, George did not have a realistic shot at this school. His numbers (his GPA and standardized test scores) put him within the *lower* range of the U Penn average. Although his application would get on the table for *consideration*—lots of applications don't even make it that far—there was nothing else in the application to get him *accepted.* His lack of leadership, community service, and extracurricular participation was a glaring weakness in his candidacy.

At this level, George would be contending with students who brought both academics on the *higher* end of the school average *and* outstanding extracurricular activities. So why would U Penn pick George? He was weaker both academically *and* non-academically. In short, he was an extremely unlikely candidate for admissions at U Penn.

More selective (Emory University)

An up-and-coming school located in Atlanta, Georgia, Emory is one of the fastest rising schools in the rankings. In the 2011 *U.S. World & News Report* rankings, Emory came in at number twenty, above schools such as UC Berkeley, UCLA and

Georgetown.[94] Emory also has a top-notch undergraduate business program, something important for George. However, Emory is not quite an Ivy League school: its admission process is not quite as selective. In fact, Emory still has a more flexible approach to admissions, appropriate to its rapidly changing reputation. This gives a student like George an advantage that he would not have at the most selective schools.

George's academic profile left him at the higher range of Emory's average. This might get him special attention because a school like Emory would be interested in boosting its overall admissions statistics by raising the academic average of its incoming freshmen.

Secondly, George's application was likely to benefit from his geographical designation. Emory is a Southern school, and so tends to draw the majority of its students from the South. With its increasing profile, Emory would probably be looking to diversify its geographical distribution with students from other regions. This could be advantageous in George's case because students from California are particularly unlikely to attend a school in Atlanta. Therefore, George's chances of admissions were higher than those of a student from the South with comparable scores— even though George's extracurricular profile was not very compelling. (Note: geography won't come into play at other schools of comparable status but different location. Schools like Boston College, NYU and Northwestern have no problem attracting students from California.)

In summary, then, George was an attractive candidate at Emory because of the combination of his above-average academic profile and his geographical designation.

---

[94] "National University Rankings 2011." *U.S. News & World Report.* 17 Aug 2010.

The UCs

The UC application process, as I've explained before, is heavily driven by quantifiable factors: GPA and standardized test scores. This is because of the sheer number of applications that the UC has to consider.

George's scores did *not* make him a likely candidate for UC Berkeley and UCLA, because these two schools typically boast the highest numerical averages of the schools that make up the UC system. However, George was an attractive candidate at all the other UCs, including UC San Diego, UC Irvine and UC Santa Barbara.

*   *   *

As I said, when I met George, he was already in his senior year. There was little he could do to make a difference to his academic profile. What he *could* do was choose which colleges he would apply to wisely, making sure he was left with several good options at the end of the year. It was also important for him to package himself as well as possible, writing well-crafted essays that would present his case to the private schools on his list.

As we saw, George did well enough to leave some excellent options for him. He could attend a top-tier private school with one of the best undergraduate business programs in the U.S. or he could get into a good UC. As it turns out, George was rejected from all the Ivy League schools he applied to, as well as Johns Hopkins, Northwestern, Berkeley and UCLA. However, he ended up fielding some great offers from schools he hadn't originally considered, including Emory and Brandeis. He also found a spot at UC San Diego and UC Irvine. He is now pursuing a BBA at Emory's top-ranked Goizueta Business School.

8.2 Jessica and Second-Tier Private Schools

Jessica never liked studying. She also didn't take on the standard range of extracurricular activities high school students typically sign up for. What Jessica really did with her time was *work*. She held down a job since sophomore year, when her father moved to Korea for his business and Jessica was exposed to the reality of her family's financial situation. Jessica spent about ten to fifteen hours per week working at the local yogurt shop during the school year, and twenty-five to thirty hours per week during her vacations. This large time commitment, combined with the fact that Jessica wasn't a naturally brilliant student, meant that although Jessica worked hard, both in and out of school, she was left with a weak academic profile.

Jessica, like George, came to me as a senior. In fact, she had already begun the process of applying to colleges. At this point, my job was to make sure Jessica would be realistic in assessing her chances and identify those colleges that would most likely value her non-academic achievements.

Highlights of Jessica's application are detailed on the next two pages. As we did with George, we'll consider how Jessica's profile would look to admissions officers at three very different kinds of colleges: top-tier and second-tier colleges, mid-tier colleges, and the UCs.

Upper-tier (first- and second-tier) private schools

Simply put, Jessica did not have a chance at this level of admissions. Her academic profile was simply too low to merit consideration and her extracurricular record did nothing to compensate for this. Jessica should not have even applied to the most selective schools. She should also have taken schools like the University of Chicago, Johns Hopkins University, even NYU off her list: she didn't have a reasonable chance of getting admitted to these schools.

Transcript

FRESHMAN YEAR		
Course	Fall Semester	Spring Semester
English	A-	B+
Health/Life Skills	A	A
Geometry	A-	B+
Biology	B	B
French 1	A	A
PE	A	A

SOPHOMORE YEAR		
Course	Fall Semester	Spring Semester
English	B	B
World History	A-	A-
Algebra 2	B	B+
Chemistry	B	B
French 2	A-	A-
PE	A	A

JUNIOR YEAR		
Course	Fall Semester	Spring Semester
English	B	B-
U.S. History	A-	B+
Trigonometry	B-	B
Physiology	A-	B+
French 3	B+	A-
Art	A-	A

Standardized Test Record:

SAT: 1720

> Math: 640
> Critical Reading: 520
> Writing: 560

Math 2: 680

Korean: 720

Extracurricular Activities:

Korean Club:
Participant (junior year)

Environmental Club:
Participant (junior year)

Job:
Supervisor of yogurt shop
(sophomore through senior year)

Recommendations:

Physiology Instructor
(junior year)

French Instructor
(junior year)

Yogurt Shop Owner

Intended Major:

Undeclared

The UCs

Furthermore, Jessica didn't have a lot of choices open to her at the UCs. Remember the UCs admissions protocol is very numbers-driven. With Jessica's low academic profile, she only had a shot at UC Riverside, UC Santa Cruz, and UC Merced.

To be clear, Jessica's application to the upper UCs wouldn't be rejected because of the lack of *rigor* in Jessica's curriculum, but because her GPA and SAT scores weren't on par with those of other applicants. AP and honors coursework is rewarded by a strict algorithmic weighting function that the UC has published. So it's *already* factored into the GPA that the UC considers. Yes, Jessica could have taken more AP and honors courses. But given her other commitments and her natural aptitude, she would in all likelihood have received no better than Cs in these advanced classes. And Cs in AP or honors classes would have been no better at the UCs than the Bs Jessica did attain in regular classes.

Mid-tier private schools

Now the beauty of U.S. college admissions is the fact that a student who might not even get into UC Riverside could still have a decent shot at getting into some private schools that are a better fit for her. Jessica's academic profile fit that of students who get accepted into schools such as Ohio Wesleyan University (OWU), a highly recommended school featured in the book *Colleges that Change Lives*.[95] In fact, OWU offers some combined-degree programs with institutions that are notoriously difficult to get into, such as Caltech. At a school like OWU, Jessica would benefit from a world-class education while finding herself in a diverse and nurturing learning environment. And a university like OWU would be much more likely to credit Jessica's impressive employment experience and the maturity she demonstrated by working from such a young age. Although

---

[95] Pope, Loren. *Colleges That Change Lives: 40 Schools That Will Change the Way You Think About Colleges.* New York: Penguin, 2006.

non-academic achievements don't play a major factor in the UC decision process, they would give Jessica a chance to shine in the more personalized and holistic admission practices of smaller, less well-known liberal arts colleges and mid-tier universities.

*   *   *

Jessica ended up with a place at UC Santa Cruz as well as two Cal State schools. However, she also had several offers from private schools, including OWU and St Mary's College in California, with generous financial aid packages that made them affordable options for her.

8.3 Luke and Harvard University

This is the story of the boy who got in. However dire the news about the increasingly competitive nature of college admissions, the fact of the matter is that students—thousands of them!—are getting accepted into the world's top universities every year. Admittedly, these students do comprise a highly select group, less than 10% of the application pool in some instances. However, in this case study, we will see that it doesn't take perfection or prodigious ability to get into a top caliber school.

Luke's details are given over the next page. But before turning to it, let's list the six elements of the college application. In order from most to least important, they are:

1. GPA
2. Standardized test scores
3. Extracurricular activities
4. Personal statement
5. Teacher recommendations
6. Interview (if required)

Transcript

FRESHMAN YEAR

Course	Fall Semester	Spring Semester
English	A	A
World History	A	A
Geometry	A-	A
Biology	A	A
French 2	A	A
Photography	A	A

SOPHOMORE YEAR

Course	Fall Semester	Spring Semester
English	A	A
U.S. Government	A	A-
Trigonometry	A-	A
Chemistry	A	A+
French 3	A	A-
Dance	A	A

JUNIOR YEAR

Course	Fall Semester	Spring Semester
Honors English	A	A
AP U.S. History	A	A-
Honors Precalculus	A	A
AP Biology	A	A-
AP French	A-	A
Honors Physics	A	A

Standardized Test Record:

SAT: 2290

> Math: 780
> Critical Reading: 760
> Writing: 750

Math 2: 800

Chemistry: 790

Chinese: 760

AP Biology: 5

AP U.S. History: 5

AP French: 3

Extracurricular Activities:

Varsity Fencing:
Nationally ranked competitor
(four years)

Youth Fencing:
Director (three years)

World Affairs Council:
Ambassador (two years)

City Youth Council:
President (four years)

Model United Nations:
Founder and President
(two years)

Big Brothers and Big Sisters:
Volunteer (four years)

Now let's briefly remember George and Jessica. George had strong academics but poor extracurricular activities. Jessica had poor academics but a strong work background. George and Jessica demonstrated weaknesses in (1), (2) and (3), and this took them out of contention at the most competitive schools. What Luke did, which neither George nor Jessica managed, was keep *all* the balls in the air.

Luke was a student at a highly regarded public school in Orange County. The school's well-known name both helps and hurts: it gives a student's academic record that much more credibility; however, the students at the school are often in direct competition with each other for coveted university spots. Typically, a school such as Luke's will send around twenty applications to Harvard every year. Harvard, obviously, can't accept twenty students, however qualified, from one school. So what made Luke's application successful?

Clearly, Luke's academic performance left little to be desired. We must note, however, that Luke's grades weren't perfect. He received an A– here and there. He also didn't retake his SAT, even though he would almost certainly have gotten a higher score. Still, Luke's numbers were good enough to put him *in the running* everywhere: they weren't good enough to *earn* him a spot at the most selective schools in and of themselves, but remember that it's not obvious that *any* grades or scores can do this. In fact, several students at Luke's school with better grades were *not* accepted to the same schools that Luke was. This is where the non-quantifiable factors of Luke's application came into play.

So let's now focus on Luke's extracurricular record. Although there were many noteworthy elements, we could point out that lots of students participate, as Luke did, in student government, and establish clubs in their schools, and engage in volunteerism. So what made Luke's application outstanding? The answer lies in the *details* of Luke's extracurricular résumé. It was exceptional in three ways:

1. Extent of volunteerism. In the interest of space, we weren't able to list the full extent of Luke's volunteer work. Needless to say, it was impressive. While maintaining his excellent school grades, Luke logged over 700 hours of volunteer work in various capacities, including mentorship and tutoring.

2. Political activism. Luke was interested in majoring in political science. Now it's one thing for a student to express an interest in politics; it's another for this passion to leap off the student's extracurricular résumé! Luke's participation in political activities, both at the local and national level, was really extensive. See how many of Luke's activities—Model U.N., World Affairs Council, City Youth Council—were driven by Luke's passion for politics? Luke's extracurricular activities formed a coherent snapshot of his extra-academic identity. Colleges got a great sense of his priorities, values, and character.

3. Fencing. Luke played a very unusual sport at the national level. His athletic prowess would appeal to schools with fencing teams, such as Harvard.

To summarize, then, Luke wasn't a Bill Gates or a Chelsea Clinton. He was a bright and talented young man who was strategic and diligent throughout his high school career. He stayed on top of his academics, and he didn't spread himself too thin—such students end up with a lot of random "filler" in their application—but rather, chose to participate extensively in those activities that were meaningful to him. And he was rewarded with early acceptance to Harvard University.

8.4 Mike and Carnegie Mellon University

Mike attended an excellent public school in northern California before heading off to Carnegie Mellon (CMU). However, as his details (given over the next two pages) show, at one point Mike's chances looked anything *but* promising.

Transcript

SOPHOMORE YEAR		
Course	Fall Semester	Spring Semester
English	B+	B
Critical Writing/Poetry	A-	A-
Honors Precalculus	B	C
Honors Chemistry	B-	B-
Japanese 1	B	C
Jazz Band	A	A
Band/Symphony	A	A

JUNIOR YEAR		
Course	Fall Semester	Spring Semester
Honors English	B	A-
AP U.S. History	B	B+
AP Calculus AB	C+	C+
Physics	B-	B
Japanese 2	C	C+
Jazz Band	A	A
Band/Symphony	A	A

SENIOR YEAR	
Course	Fall Semester
AP English	A
Government/ Economics	A
AP Statistics	A
Physiology	A
Japanese 3	A
Jazz Band	A

Standardized Test Record:

SAT (June 2009): 2100

> Math: 700
> Critical Reading: 700
> Writing: 700

SAT (Oct 2009): 2100

> Math: 700
> Critical Reading: 800
> Writing: 600

Math 2: 700

Literature: 730

Chinese: 760

AP Calculus AB: 3

AP U.S. History: 4

Extracurricular Activities:

Marching Band:
Section Leader
(junior and senior year)

Volunteer Work:
Intermittent participation
(junior and senior year)

Mike's parents brought him to me because they were worried about whether Mike would get into *any* college! Mike's sophomore- and junior-year transcript was littered with Bs and Cs. The only As on his record were in courses that he liked, such as poetry and band.

Obviously Mike's transcript wasn't his strong point. Fortunately, his standardized test scores were a bright spot. They were strong enough to demonstrate Mike's ability to do college level work. But in fact, they were also higher than the average for Carnegie Mellon: CMU super-scores the SATs, so Mike's SAT score was considered a 2200.

Another thing Mike had going for him was his extensive participation in marching band. Colleges understand how much of a time commitment marching band is. In the first semester of the school year, band easily took up twenty to twenty-five hours of Mike's week (twelve hours on Saturdays).

Although Mike's application had its strengths, if his story ended right after his junior year, Mike *definitely* wouldn't have gotten into CMU. (For that matter, he wouldn't have gotten into many schools that are less selective than CMU.) So how did Mike pull this off?

Everything turned on his senior-year grades. After Mike and his families had a frank discussion with me, Mike decided to get serious about his academics. Many students make this sort of promise flippantly, without making any of the real changes necessary to achieving their goals. However, Mike really found the discipline and made an *extremely* impressive turnaround. He achieved straight As during *the* most difficult semester of high school, all while studying for the SAT and writing college essays and *without* giving up on any of his other commitments, like his time-consuming marching band section leadership.

Because of his extraordinary performance senior fall, Mike was able to allay any fears that he wasn't really ready to handle college work. See, because of Mike's high standardized test scores, his intelligence was never in question. Rather, admissions officers would have been worried about his maturity and his attitude. Would he slack off? Would he be placed on academic probation? Would he flunk out, costing the college both money and resources? Mike's senior-year grades made it possible for colleges to let go of these concerns.

Mike's application to CMU was also helped, however, by CMU's commitment to attracting a diverse undergraduate population. As a school known mainly for its science and engineering programs—especially its computer science program—CMU is invested in improving its reputation in the humanities. The fact that Mike packaged himself as a humanities major helped his application, maybe significantly.

While Mike was a special case and not everyone with similar statistics can't expect similar results, students should take comfort in knowing that schools, especially private schools, are willing to take a chance on some students. Students with poor application profiles should know that there is almost always *something* they can do to help themselves. Sometimes, in fact, students can dramatically change their options if they are only willing to put in the time and effort.

8.5 Jennifer and USC (but not CMU)

Let's now compare Jennifer to Michael. Jennifer did *not* get into CMU. Let's try to figure out why.

Why Jennifer was not accepted into CMU

Like so many children of immigrants, Jennifer took a very rigorous course load. However, due to the challenging nature of her schoolwork, she earned more Bs than was ideal for a school of CMU's caliber. In other words, her school GPA was lower than that of the average CMU student. And Jennifer's standardized test scores, though excellent, were not enough to compensate for her grades.

Transcript

SOPHOMORE YEAR		
Course	Fall Semester	Spring Semester
English	A-	A-
World History/ Government	A-	B+
Algebra 2/ Trigonometry	A-	A-
Honors Chemistry	B-	B-
Journalism/ Art	B-	B+
Japanese 2	B-	B+

JUNIOR YEAR		
Course	Fall Semester	Spring Semester
English	A	A-
AP U.S. History	B-	B
Precalculus	A	A-
AP Biology	B	B
Physics	A	A
Japanese 3	B+	A-

SENIOR YEAR	
Course	Fall Semester
English	A
AP Economics	B
AP Calculus AB	A-
AP Statistics	B
AP Psychology	A
AP Japanese	A

Standardized Test Record:

SAT: 2190

    Math: 780
    Critical Reading: 720
    Writing: 690

Math 2: 800

World History: 620

Biology: 710

U.S. History: 690

AP Calculus AB: 3

AP U.S. History: 4

Extracurricular Activities:

Violin:
5th-11th grade

California Youth Symphony:
Member, 8th - 11th grade

School Badminton:
Participant
(sophomore and junior year)

Magic Club:
Vice-President
(sophomore year)

Key Club:
Member (three years)

Writing:
Drafting a fantasy novel;
150 pages so far

Now the same could be said of Michael, who, remember, *was* accepted into CMU. He also had lower grades and a high SAT score. However, Michael's profile was different in three notable ways:

1. Michael's transcript documented a remarkable rise in scores his senior year. Jennifer's GPA, by contrast, while never particularly low any given semester, also never showed any notable improvement. There was no evidence that Jennifer *could* do better, given greater motivation or more focus.

2. Michael's extracurricular record, although not broad, was deep: he didn't participate in a whole lot of activities, but he demonstrated a long-term commitment to marching band, an extremely time-consuming activity in which he assumed a leadership role. Jennifer, on the other hand, didn't show any particular commitment in any of her activities. She participated in a variety of activities (music, sports, clubs), but started and stopped them at whim. Her profile was too scattered; it's impossible to see what she is really passionate about.

3. Finally, Michael applied to CMU as a humanities student, but Jennifer applied as a computer science major. Computer science is one of the school's most popular majors. Because CMU is particularly well known for its science and engineering programs, it has no problem attracting major talent in that area. Getting into the CMU College of Computer Science is much harder than getting into the CMU College of Humanities and Social Sciences.

Why Jennifer was accepted into the University of Southern California

Now let's see why Jennifer was accepted into the University of Southern California (USC). Simply put, the answer lies in numbers. Jennifer got into USC because her academic averages and standardized test scores were significantly higher than the

USC average. This made up for the fact that she lacked a strong extracurricular profile. In fact, USC gave her a substantial scholarship.

*　　*　　*

Comparing Michael and Jennifer illustrates why admissions is as much an art as a science. It's impossible to predict where a student will get in based on numbers alone. A whole variety of factors come into play: extracurricular activities, intended major, and a whole host of other non-quantifiable factors.

8.6　Jamie and the Ivy League

The statistics are grim. Students accepted to the Harvard Class of 2014 were a *highly* select few: only 2,150 made the cut from over 30,000 applications received, a 7% acceptance rate.[96] Same for the Yale Class of 2014: 1,950 candidates were accepted out of 25,800 applications (roughly 7.5%).[97] Stanford, too, accepted only 7% of applicants (as compared to 9.5% in previous years).[98] With the number of applications rising every year and the percentage of acceptances dropping each year, many students and parents are well justified in feeling frustrated. How do the lucky few do it? What really gets a student accepted into an Ivy League or similar caliber school?

Let's take a look at Jamie, who attended a highly ranked public school in northern California. She was accepted into top Ivy-League schools: Harvard, Yale and Stanford. How did she do it? Here are her achievements:

---

[96] Wickett, Shana. "Good Luck! – You'll Need It; Harvard Applications Set New Record." *Boston Globe.* 14 Jan 2010.

[97] Lu, Carmen. "Fall in Applications Defies Trend." *Yale Daily News.* 22 Jan 2010.

[98] Hoover, Eric. "Application Inflation: When Is Enough Enough?" *New York Times.* 05 Nov 2010.

Transcript

SOPHOMORE YEAR		
Course	**Fall Semester**	**Spring Semester**
Honors English	A	A
AP European History	A	A
Honors Precalculus	A	A
AP Chemistry	A	A
Spanish 3	A	A
AP Art History	A	A
PE	A	A

JUNIOR YEAR		
Course	**Fall Semester**	**Spring Semester**
AP English Language	A	A
AP U.S. History	A	A
AP Calculus AB	A	A
AP Environmental Science	A	A
AP Spanish	A	A
Journalism	A	A

SENIOR YEAR	
Course	**Fall Semester**
AP English Literature	A
AP Government	A
AP Statistics	A
AP Biology	A
Journalism	A

Standardized Test Record:

SAT: 2230

>   Math: 760
>   Critical Reading: 770
>   Writing: 700

Math 2: 800

U.S. History: 800

Chemistry: 800

AP European History: 5

AP Chemistry: 4

AP Art History: 5

AP U.S. History: 5

AP Calculus AB: 5

AP Environmental Science: 5

AP Spanish: 5

AP English Language: 5

Select Extracurricular Activities:

Three-week HIV Awareness Journalism Project in Ghana

Four-week Chemical Analysis Internship: with Dow Chemical

Environmental Club: President

Varsity Golf: Member (four years)

Journalism: Editor (two years)

Volunteer Work: Hospital (four years)

Piano and Violin

Now let's analyze this data. Jamie's academic record speaks for itself. She maintained a perfect GPA while taking an ambitious course load. She had near perfect standardized test scores. However, these numbers alone don't explain Jamie's admissions success. Why? Believe it or not, there are simply too many students with even better academic profiles every year. With such talented scholars in their admissions pools, the most selective colleges can be extremely picky. In fact, notice that Jamie's academic record wasn't perfect. She didn't take the *most* challenging classes: she skipped AP Calculus BC and AP Physics. In addition, her SAT score, while excellent, could have been higher. In short, Jamie was certainly up against students with even *more* impressive academic records. So how did Jamie get in?

First of all, her academic profile was good enough. Remember, numbers are only part of the admissions process. Colleges are looking for a certain level of ability, after which little distinctions— say, between a 2300 and a 2350 on the SAT—don't really matter. Surprisingly, some of the weaknesses in Jamie's record may have helped her. The fact that she didn't retake the SAT demonstrated that she wasn't overly focused on a test that most colleges consider a necessary evil. The fact that she didn't take certain AP math and science classes fit the profile of a student who, while not shying away from challenges, tailored her studies around her genuine interests.

Jamie also had clearly defined passions. She had two areas of keen interest, journalism and medical volunteer work, and she pursued these with tenacity. But her passions were attested to by more than the *quantity* of time she devoted. They were better demonstrated by the *quality* of her activities. Note that lots of Jamie's school-year activities, such as her hospital work and her position on the school paper, are very common. But Jamie connected these activities with big summer projects, like the HIV Awareness Journalism Project in Ghana. She demonstrated a level of initiative far beyond what most participants are able to achieve.

Jamie was also able to achieve balance. Although she clearly had priorities, she was able to juggle multiple commitments with a rich extracurricular life. She excelled in academics, volunteer work, music and sports. (Notice that her athletic ability, while not a primary strength, still showed character.)

Finally, Jamie wrote a thoughtful college essay about her experiences in Ghana. Although excellent essays alone won't get students into a school, it can push one candidate out from among a pile of equally qualified candidates. Jamie's essay succeeded in this regard. It provided what was just a list of achievements with a personality, identity and voice.

It's not surprising that, with all these achievements, Jamie was able to get into some of the most selective colleges in the world. What might be a bit more surprising is that Jamie chose to attend Amherst College, a small, highly exclusive liberal arts college, over Stanford, Harvard, and Yale. Jamie's goal was to become a doctor, and she felt that Amherst would be the best path to this goal. In making this decision, Jamie displayed just the same kind of independence, maturity, and wisdom that got her into every college she applied to.

Remember that Jamie wasn't a prodigy: not in school, nor on the athletic field, nor on the concert stage. She was a very intelligent student who pursued what she loved with dedication, initiative and integrity. In the next section, we'll compare Jamie with Sarah, another, equally talented student who did *not* get into the same schools Jamie was accepted at.

8.7 Sarah and the Ivy League

For every "Jamie," there are thousands of superficially similar students who do *not* get accepted. Why? This section profiles one of Jamie's classmates. While Sarah was accepted to Columbia, U Penn, Brown, Cornell, MIT and Northwestern, she was *not* accepted to Stanford, Harvard, Yale or Princeton.

Transcript

SOPHOMORE YEAR		
Course	Fall Semester	Spring Semester
Honors English	A	A
Honors World History	A	A
AP Calculus BC	A	A
AP Chemistry	A	A
Spanish 3	A	A
Honors Physics	A	A
PE	A	A

JUNIOR YEAR		
Course	Fall Semester	Spring Semester
AP English Language	A	A
AP U.S. History	A	A
College Math	A	A
AP Physics	A	A
Honors Spanish 4	A	A
Computer Programming	A	A

SENIOR YEAR	
Course	Fall Semester
AP English Literature	A
AP Government	A
College Math	A
AP Biology	A
AP Spanish	A
Web Design	A

Standardized Test Record:

SAT: 2370

> Math: 800
> Critical Reading: 770
> Writing: 800

Math 2: 800

Physics: 800

Chemistry: 800

AP Physics: 5

AP Chemistry: 5

AP Calculus BC: 5

AP U.S. History: 5

AP Biology: 5

AP English Language: 5

AP Government: 5

AP Spanish: 5

Select Extracurricular Activities:

U.S. Math Olympiad:
National Quarter-Finalist

Math Club: Treasurer
(four years)

Softball Team: Participant
(three years)

Volunteer Work: Hospital
(four years)

City Youth Council: Member

Now let's analyze this data. Sarah's academic record, like Jamie's, was virtually flawless. She maintained a perfect GPA while taking a very ambitious course load. She had near perfect standardized test scores. Remember, however, that academics alone are never enough. They don't guarantee any student admission to a top private school. In fact, Sarah is the perfect example of just this very point.

Of course, we need to maintain perspective. Although Sarah didn't get into Harvard, Stanford, Yale or Princeton, she did get accepted into all the other schools on her list, including several Ivy League schools. In no sense was Sarah a failure; she racked up a *highly* impressive record of admissions. Still, in this section I'm going to see what set Jamie apart from Sarah. What makes the difference at the highest level of achievement and competitiveness?

First, let's consider the major strength of Sarah's application. One factor was obviously instrumental in gaining Sarah admissions from a good number of very selective colleges: Sarah's academic profile. Although numbers are only one part of the admissions process, Sarah's GPA and SAT scores were *particularly* remarkable. She also demonstrated unusual—even for Ivy standards—strengths in math and science, completing AP Calculus BC her sophomore year and continuing to develop her interest by taking math classes at the college level. In addition, Sarah took every single AP science available to her. In Sarah's case, even more than in Jamie's, it's hard to say how anyone could have achieved more academically.

So why didn't Sarah get in? Let's consider the weaknesses of Sarah's application.

1. Sarah had no clearly defined passion. Remember, Jamie's commitment to journalism and medically-based volunteer work leapt off the page. Sarah had no such obvious passion. Her activities didn't create a compelling profile of her extracurricular interests. They re-emphasized Sarah's interest in math and science, but

didn't provide admissions officers with anything new to hook onto.

2. Sarah had no leadership experience and there was nothing qualitatively distinct about her extracurricular record. Notice that although both Jamie and Sarah participated in hospital volunteer work, Jamie's hospital work took on a much greater significance: Jamie integrated her interest in health-related issues with her interest in journalism and found the initiative to get all the way to Ghana. Sarah's interest in health issues was obviously not nearly as strong.

3. Finally, Jamie was able to talk about her unique experience in Ghana in her essay. Her topic alone helped her stand out. Sarah, by contrast, didn't have any compelling experiences to share. And she was unable to find a way to take one of the experiences she *did* have and narrate it in a new and revealing way. Sarah ended up with a fairly common essay about learning to manage her own perfectionism.

Now this section is certainly not intended to discredit Sarah's impressive achievements or discourage readers with stories of impressive individuals who didn't make it into the very top universities. However, as a college counselor, it's frustrating to see individuals with all the ability, motivation and skill to get into a university fail to secure admissions because of a lack of information. The right message at the right time might have encouraged Sarah to step outside of her safety zone and take a few risks; it might have led her to discover a really compelling passion; it might have given her that last push she needed to get into those last exclusive universities.

*   *   *

I hope all my readers have found someone to learn from and someone to inspire them in these pages. Some of my readers may be motivated by Mike to finally attain the discipline and integrity necessary to achieve their academic potential. Some might be motivated by Sarah to find the freedom and courage to do what they're passionate about.

Let me close by assuring all of my readers: the right college is out there. It may take a lot of self-reflection to find it. And it will take a lot of hard work and careful planning to get to it. But until applications are in, it's neither too early nor too late to do *something* to get one step closer.

Conclusion

In conclusion, I'll list the five most important things that I hope families facing the college admissions process take away from this book.

1. *There is no one "right" way to get into college.* Every student must travel a different path, because getting into college is essentially a matter of discovering strengths, identifying passions, developing character... in short, becoming an adult.

2. *Students must meet minimal academic criteria in order to even be* considered *at a school.* No matter how fantastic a student's activities, a college will *not* accept a student who is not able to succeed academically on campus. Students *must* make sure that they do not pin their hopes and energies on schools where they won't even make it past the first hurdle.

3. *Every school has a different "culture," just as every student has a different personality.* A student might be admitted to MIT but not to Princeton, not because the student isn't qualified to succeed at Princeton, but because he or she fits in better with the culture at MIT. Or one applicant might get admitted to Yale while another with equivalent academic achievements is not, because the first student demonstrates a kind of social

mindedness that fits in better with Yale's values and ethos. Finding the right fit between college and student is a complex process. In order to give themselves the best shot, students should adopt a coherent application strategy, one that puts their unique identities clearly on display.

4. *Colleges don't just want smart students. They want* good *students.* They want students with strength of character, who will make a positive impact on the community. This is why colleges value leadership, initiative and community engagement.

5. *It's crucial for students, whatever stage of the process they're in, to develop a vision* now *and start acting on it so as not to close any doors or miss any opportunities.*

Even for the best prepared, most gifted students, the college admissions process is never going to be anything other than highly stressful! However, with the right information and with careful planning, the process is certainly manageable. It can even be deeply meaningful.

This book has cataloged the most important things college-bound students from immigrant families should know about each element of the college application and every step of the college admissions process. The facts and case studies presented here should help every student reading this book secure the best possible opportunities for themselves. Now it is up to the student to find the motivation and drive to take control of the future.

Appendix I: Top Fifty Universities[99]

1. Harvard University (Cambridge, MA)
2. Princeton University (Princeton, NJ)
3. Yale University (New Haven, CT)
4. Columbia University (New York, NY)
5. Stanford University (Stanford, CA)
5. University of Pennsylvania (Philadelphia, PA)
7. California Institute of Technology (Pasadena, CA)
7. Massachusetts Institute of Technology (Cambridge, MA)
9. Dartmouth College (Hanover, NH)
9. Duke University (Durham, NC)
9. University of Chicago (Chicago, IL)
12. Northwestern University (Evanston, IL)
13. Johns Hopkins University (Baltimore, MD)
13. Washington University in St. Louis (St. Louis, MO)
15. Brown University (Providence, RI)
15. Cornell University (Ithaca, NY)
17. Rice University (Houston, TX)
18. Vanderbilt University (Nashville, TN)
19. University of Notre Dame (Notre Dame, IN)
20. Emory University (Atlanta, GA)
21. Georgetown University (Washington, DC)
22. UC Berkeley (Berkeley, CA)
23. Carnegie Mellon University (Pittsburgh, PA)
23. University of Southern California (Los Angeles, CA)
25. UCLA (Los Angeles, CA)
25. University of Virginia (Charlottesville, VA)
25. Wake Forest University (Winston-Salem, NC)
28. Tufts University (Medford, MA)
29. University of Michigan, Ann Arbor (Ann Arbor, MI)
30. University of North Carolina, Chapel Hill (Chapel Hill, NC)
31. Boston College (Chestnut Hill, MA)

---

[99] "National University Rankings 2011." *U.S. News & World Report.* 17 Aug 2010.

31. College of William & Mary (Williamsburg, VA)
33. New York University (New York, NY)
34. Brandeis University (Waltham, MA)
35. Georgia Institute of Technology (Atlanta, GA)
35. UC San Diego (La Jolla, CA)
37. Lehigh University (Bethlehem, PA)
37. University of Rochester (Rochester, NY)
39. UC Davis (Davis, CA)
39. UC Santa Barbara (Santa Barbara, CA)
41. Case Western Reserve University (Cleveland, OH)
41. Rensselaer Polytechnic Institute (Troy, NY)
41. UC Irvine (Irvine, CA)
41. University of Washington (Seattle, WA)
45. University of Texas, Austin (Austin, TX)
45. University of Wisconsin, Madison (Madison, WI)
47. Pennsylvania State University, University Park (University Park, PA)
47. University of Illinois, Urbana-Champaign (Champaign, IL)
47. University of Miami (Coral Gables, FL)
50. Yeshiva University (New York, NY)

Appendix II:
Top Fifty Public Universities[100]

1. UC Berkeley (rank 22)
2. UCLA (rank 25)
3. University of Virginia (rank 25)
4. University of Michigan, Ann Arbor (rank 29)
5. University of North Carolina, Chapel Hill (rank 30)
6. College of William and Mary (rank 31)
7. Georgia Institute of Technology (rank 35)
8. UC San Diego (rank 35)
9. UC Davis (rank 39)
10. UC Santa Barbara (rank 39)
11. UC Irvine (rank 41)
12. University of Washington (rank 41)
13. University of Texas, Austin (rank 45)
14. University of Wisconsin, Madison (rank 45)
15. Pennsylvania State University, University Park (rank 47)
16. University of Illinois, Urbana-Champaign (rank 47)
17. University of Florida (rank 53)
18. Ohio State University, Columbus (rank 56)
19. Purdue University, West Lafayette (rank 56)
20. University of Georgia (rank 56)
21. University of Maryland, College Park (rank 56)
22. Texas A&M University, College Station (rank 63)
23. Clemson University (rank 64)
24. Rutgers State University of New Jersey, New Brunswick (rank 64)
25. University of Minnesota, Twin Cities (rank 64)
26. University of Pittsburgh (rank 64)
27. University of Connecticut (rank 69)
28. Virginia Tech (rank 69)
29. Colorado School of Mines (rank 72)
30. UC Santa Cruz (rank 72)
31. University of Iowa (rank 72)
32. Indiana University, Bloomington (rank 75)
33. University of Delaware (rank 75)

---

[100] "Top Public Schools 2011." *U.S. News & World Report.* 17 Aug 2010.

34. Miami University, Oxford (rank 79)
35. Michigan State University (rank 79)
36. State University of New York, College of Environmental Science and Forestry (rank 79)
37. University of Alabama (rank 79)
38. Auburn University (rank 85)
39. State University of New York, Binghamton (rank 86)
40. University of Colorado, Boulder (rank 86)
41. Iowa State University (rank 94)
42. UC Riverside (rank 94)
43. University of Missouri (rank 94)
44. University of Vermont (rank 94)
45. State University of New York, Stonybrook (rank 99)
46. University of Massachusetts, Amherst (rank 99)
47. Florida State University (rank 104)
48. University of Kansas (rank 104)
49. University of Nebraska, Lincoln (rank 104)
50. University of New Hampshire (rank 104)

Appendix III:
Top Fifty Liberal Arts Colleges[101]

1. Williams College (Williamstown, MA)
2. Amherst College (Amherst, MA)
3. Swarthmore College (Swarthmore, PA)
4. Middlebury College (Middlebury, VT)
4. Wellesley College (Wellesley, MA)
6. Bowdoin College (Brunswick, ME)
6. Pomona College (Claremont, CA)
8. Carleton College (Northfield, MN)
9. Davidson College (Davidson, NC)
9. Haverford College (Haverford, PA)
11. Claremont McKenna College (Claremont, CA)
12. Vassar College (Poughkeepsie, NY)
12. Wesleyan University (Middletown, CT)
14. Smith College (Northampton, MA)
14. Washington and Lee University (Lexington, VA)
16. United States Military Academy (West Point, NY)
16. United States Naval Academy (Annapolis, MD)
18. Grinnell College (Grinnell, IA)
18. Hamilton College (Clinton, NY)
18. Harvey Mudd College (Claremont, CA)
21. Bates College (Lewiston, ME)
21. Colgate University (Hamilton, NY)
23. Colby College (Waterville, ME)
23. Oberlin College (Oberlin, OH)
23. Scripps College (Claremont, CA)
26. Barnard College (New York, NY)
26. Colorado College (Colorado Springs, CO)
26. Macalester College (St. Paul, MN)
26. Mount Holyoke College (South Hadley, MA)
30. Bryn Mawr College (Bryn Mawr, PA)

---

[101] "National Liberal Arts College Rankings 2011." *U.S. News & World Report.* 17 Aug 2010.

30. Bucknell University
    (Lewisburg, PA)
32. College of the Holy Cross
    (Worcester, MA)
32. Kenyon College
    (Gambier, OH)
32. Sewanee,
    University of the South
    (Sewanee, TN)
32. University of Richmond
    (Richmond, VA)
36. Occidental College
    (Los Angeles, CA)
36. Trinity College
    (Hartford, CT)
38. Bard College (Annandale
    on Hudson, NY)
38. Lafayette College
    (Easton, PA)
38. Whitman College
    (Walla Walla, WA)
41. Connecticut College
    (New London, CT)
41. Franklin and Marshall
    College (Lancaster, PA)
41. Furman University
    (Greenville, SC)
41. Skidmore College
    (Saratoga Springs, NY)
41. Union College
    (Schenectady, NY)
46. Pitzer College (Claremont,
    CA)
47. Centre College
    (Danville, KY)
47. Dickinson College (Carlisle,
    PA)
47. Gettysburg College
    (Gettysburg, PA)

47. Rhodes College
    (Memphis, TN)

Appendix IV: About the Rankings

The *U.S. News & World Report*'s annual ranking of universities and colleges is always big news. Everyone knows about these tables; and everyone—even vocal critics of the table's principles and methodology—cares about where their college or alma mater placed in the most recent tables. But very few people know how these rankings are generated. Here's a quick primer.

The rankings are generated by assigning a value to a school's performance along seven different axes of evaluation, and then weighting these values in accordance with the following percentages:

- Peer assessment: 25%

- Graduation and retention rates: 20%

- Faculty resources: 20%

- Student selectivity: 15%

- Financial resources: 10%

- Alumni giving: 5%

- Graduation rate performance: 5%[102]

Now clearly, one of the things that a college can most directly improve is the student selectivity rating. Colleges can't make their alumni give more money (although climbing in the rankings sure seems to open pockets)! Nor can colleges force their undergraduates to finish within four years (although they can make it easier or harder for students to do so). But colleges *can* increase student selectivity.

What exactly falls under the rubric, "student selectivity"? Numbers such as the percentage of incoming freshmen who graduated in the top 10% of their high school; the average SAT

---

[102] "How *U.S. News* Calculates the College Rankings." *U.S. News & World Report*. 17 Aug 2010.

or ACT performance of matriculating freshmen; and the percentage of applicants accepted.

Now remember that GPA is the number one factor governing college admissions. A stellar GPA is a *minimum* condition for receiving serious consideration at the most selective schools. But it isn't *sufficient* for getting in: no transcript, however remarkable, will be enough, simply because when a college is only admitting around 7% of all applicants, *it is turning away too many students with perfect transcripts.*

But for other schools in the top tier, a stellar GPA *can* make the difference. It can get a student in, not just on the table. Why? Because accepting students with exceptional academic achievements—even if these students don't bring much else with them—is one of the most straightforward ways for these colleges to improve their rankings.

Details aside, the take-home message is simple. For students targeting *any* of the schools in the top tier, whether the top two (Harvard and Princeton) or the bottom two (Emory and Notre Dame), a strong GPA must take top priority.